The Wit and Wisdom of
ABRAHAM LINCOLN

Compiled and Edited by
Bill Adler

A Citadel Press Book
Published by Carol Publishing Group

A Citadel Press Book
Published by Carol Publishing Group
Citadel Press is a registered trademark of Carol Communications, Inc.
Editorial Offices: 600 Madison Avenue, New York, N.Y. 10022
Sales and Distribution Offices: 120 Enterprise Avenue, Secaucus, N.J. 07094
In Canada: Canadian Manda Group, P.O. Box 920, Station U, Toronto, Ontario M8Z 5P9
Queries regarding rights and permissions should be addressed to Carol Publishing Group, 600 Madison Avenue, New York, N.Y. 10022

Carol Publishing Group books are available at special discounts for bulk purchases, for sales promotion, fund-raising, or educational purposes. Special editions can be created to specifications. For details, contact: Special Sales Department, Carol Publishing Group, 120 Enterprise Avenue, Secaucus, N.J. 07094

Manufactured in the United States of America
10 9 8 7 6 5 4 3 2 1

Library of Congress Cataloging-in-Publication Data

Lincoln, Abraham, 1809-1865.
    The wit and wisdom of Abraham Lincoln / compiled and edited by Bill Adler.
        p.   cm.
    "A Citadel Press book."
    ISBN 0-8065-1456-6
    1. Lincoln, Abraham, 1809-1865—Humor.   2. Lincoln, Abraham,
1809-1865—Philosophy.   I. Adler, Bill, 1956-   .   II. Title.
E457.2.W78, 1993
973.7'092—dc20   93-27950
CIP

We are most grateful to Virginia Fay for
her creative assistance in the preparation
of this book.

CONTENTS

ANIMALS

A garrulous politician reminded Lincoln of a peacock he had seen on a farm in Kentucky: "That's a fine bird," the owner suggested. Lincoln: "Yes, he's a very pretty bird, and if he would only keep his mouth shut, people would never know what a blamed old fool he is."

❖ ❖ ❖

Regarding the Trent Affair:

"I remember when I was a lad, there were two fields behind our house separated by a fence. In each field there was a big bulldog, and these dogs spent the whole day racing up and down, snarling and yelping at each other through that fence. One day they both came at the same moment to a hole in it, big enough to let either of them through. Well, gentlemen, what do you think they did? They just turned tail and scampered away as fast as they could in opposite directions. Now, England and America are like those bulldogs."

❖ ❖ ❖

Lincoln was thankful to Conant (the painter) for one thing: the Slow Horse Story:

"A politician went to a livery stable [the story ran] for a horse to drive sixteen miles to a convention where he wanted the nomination for county judge. The horse broke down, he arrived late, lost the nomination, and came back to the livery stable feeling it was useless to be angry. He said to the liveryman, 'See here, Jones. You are training this horse for the New York market. You expect to sell him for a good price to an undertaker for a hearse horse.' But Jones insisted the horse was one of the best in his stable. 'Now don't deny it,' said the

1

politician, 'for I know by his gait that you have spent a great deal of time training him to go before a hearse. But he will never do. He is so slow he couldn't get a corpse to the cemetery in time for the resurrection.' "

❋   ❋   ❋

A man came to a farm to have a look at a rare specimen of a big hog. The farmer insisted on charging twenty-five cents for the look. The stranger paid the two bits and started walking away. The farmer called, "Don't you want to see the hog?" "No, I've seen as big a hog as I care to see for today."

❋   ❋   ❋

On one of Sheridan's forays, crossing the Pamunkey River near the White House, a pack mule fell off a bridge thirty feet above the water, turned a full somersault, struck an abutment, hit the water, went under, came up, swam ashore, and rejoined the troop column. Lincoln in the course of the war felt the Union cause occasionally had that mule's luck.

❋   ❋   ❋

An Ohio admirer presented Lincoln with a whistle made of a pig's tail. He blew into it, found it whistled, and laughed. "I never suspected there was music in such a thing as that."

THE ARMY

"Sending men to that army is like shoveling fleas across a barnyard—not half of them get there."

❉ ❉ ❉

"If I gave McClellan all the men he asks for they could not find room to lie down. They'd have to sleep standing up."

❉ ❉ ❉

Of a Union and Confederate army maneuvering as if they might soon fight, but not quite reaching the combat stage, he remarked that they were like "two dogs that get less eager to fight the nearer they come to each other."

❉ ❉ ❉

A woman demanded a colonel's commission for her son, not as a favor but as a right. "Sir, my grandfather fought at Lexington, my father fought at New Orleans, and my husband was killed at Monterey." Lincoln dismissed her with, "I guess, Madam, your family has done enough for the country. It is time to give someone else a chance."

❉ ❉ ❉

Nov. 11, 1863

Hon. Secretary of War.
My dear Sir:
I personally wish Jacob R. Freese, of New Jersey, to be appointed a colonel for a colored regiment—and this regardless of whether he can tell the exact shade of Julius Caesar's hair. Yours.

❉ ❉ ❉

On the winding dark staircase of the War Department building, a young officer carrying reports to Stanton rushed along

3

one evening taking three steps at a time, and butted his head with full force into the President's body at about the point of the lower vest pocket. Seeing whom he had hit, he groaned, "Ten thousand pardons." Lincoln responded: "One's enough, I wish the whole army could charge like that."

✿ ✿ ✿

The President once said he could understand the man "overcome by a physical fear greater than his will." Neither privates nor generals came in for blame in Lincoln's reply to Congressman H. C. Deming of Connecticut, who asked at which point the war might have ended if commanders had managed better. There were three such points, the President believed: "At Malvern Hill, when McClellan failed to command an immediate advance upon Richmond; at Chancellorsville, when Hooker failed to reinforce Sedgwick, after hearing his cannon upon the extreme right; and at Gettysburg, when Meade failed to attack Lee in the retreat at the bend of the Potomac." The Congressman expected denunciation or complaint or censure. Instead Lincoln further clarified: "I do not know that I could have given any different orders had I been with them myself. I have not fully made up my mind how I should behave when minie-balls were whistling, and those great oblong shells shrieking in my ear. I might run away."

✿ ✿ ✿

Lincoln gave his personal attention to the camps around Washington. He rode in an open hack with Seward across the Potomac. Colonel William Tecumseh Sherman asked if they were going to his camp. "Yes," said Lincoln. "We heard that you had got over the big scare, and we thought we would come over and see the boys."

On the way to the camp Sherman advised Lincoln to "please discourage all cheering, noise, or any sort of confusion; we had enough of it before Bull Run to spoil any set of men; what we need is cool, thoughtful, hard-fighting soldiers—no more hur-

4

rahing, no more humbug." At the camp, noted Sherman, "Mr. Lincoln stood up and made one of the neatest, best, and most feeling addresses I ever listened to, referring to our disaster, the high duties that still devolved on us, and the brighter days to come."

At one or two points the soldiers began to cheer. Lincoln checked them, "Don't cheer, boys. I confess I rather like it myself, but Colonel Sherman here says it is not military, and I guess we had better defer to his opinion."

THE CABINET

On Secretary of the Treasury Salmon P. Chase:

"Chase is a very able man. He is a very ambitious man and I think on the subject of the presidency a little insane. He has not always behaved very well lately and people say to me, 'Now is the time to crush him out.' Well, I'm not in favor of crushing anybody out! If there is anything that a man can do and do it well, I say let him do it. Give him a chance."

        ✿   ✿   ✿

"I do not see that I am exclusively responsible," Lincoln said. "I say to these gentlemen, 'Go to Secretary Chase; he is managing the finances.' They persist, and have argued me almost blind. I am worse off than St. Paul. He was in a strait betwixt two. I am in a strait betwixt twenty, and they are bankers and financiers."

        ✿   ✿   ✿

When asked what he would do about Chase's ambition to become President, he responded with a story of how he and his brother were once plowing with a lazy horse:

"On reaching the end of the furrow, I found an enormous chin-fly fastened upon [the horse], and knocked him off. My brother asked me what I did that for. I told him I didn't want the old horse bitten in that way. 'Why,' said my brother, 'that's all that made him go.'

"Now, if Mr. Chase has a Presidential chin-fly biting him, I'm not going to knock him off, if it will only make his department go."

        ✿   ✿   ✿

To the Illinois Congressman Shelby M. Cullom came a report that when Chase's letters containing mean insinuations about

Lincoln were offered for the President's reading, he commented, "If Mr. Chase has said some hard things about me, I in turn have said some hard things about him, which, I guess, squares the account." Likewise on a similar occasion: "I know meaner things about Mr. Chase than any of these men can tell me."

✿　✿　✿

On appointing Chase to Chief Justice:

"Although I may have appeared to you and to Mr. Sumner to have been opposed to Chase's appointment, there never has been a moment since the breath left old Taney's body that I did not conceive it to be the best thing to do to appoint Mr. Chase to that high office; and to have done otherwise I should have been recreant to my convictions of duty to the Republican party and to the country." Alley repeated that the action was magnanimous and patriotic. Lincoln: "As to his talk about me, I do not mind that. Chase is, on the whole, a pretty good fellow and a very able man. His only trouble is that he has 'the White House fever' a little too bad, but I hope this may cure him and that he will be satisfied."

✿　✿　✿

Commenting to a cabinet member on how he and Secretary of War Edwin Stanton got along, Lincoln said: "I cannot always know whether a permit ought to be granted, and I want to oblige everybody when I can; and Stanton and I have an understanding that if I send an order to him that cannot be consistently granted, he is to refuse it, which he sometimes does. And that led to a remark which I made the other day to a man who complained of Stanton, that I hadn't much influence with this administration, but expected to have more with the next."

✿　✿　✿

A plan for mingling Eastern and Western troops was urged on Lincoln by a committee headed by Owen Lovejoy of Illinois.

Lincoln wrote a note to Secretary Stanton suggesting a transfer of regiments. "Did Lincoln give you an order of that kind?" asked the Secretary.

"He did, sir," replied Lovejoy.

"Then he is a damned fool!" said Stanton.

"Do you mean to say the President is a damned fool?"

"Yes, sir, if he gave you such an order as that."

At the White House Lovejoy told what happened. "Did Stanton say I was a damned fool?" asked Lincoln.

"He did, sir, and repeated it."

The President was thoughtful. "If Stanton said I was a damned fool then I must be one. For he is nearly always right, and generally says what he means. I will step over and see him."

❊　❊　❊

Jany. 1, 1863

Hon. Sec. of War:

Dear Sir:

Yesterday a piteous appeal was made to me by an old lady of genteel appearance, saying she had, with what she thought sufficient assurance that she would not be disturbed by the government, fitted up the two south divisions of the old "Duff Green" building in order to take boarders, and has boarders already in it, and others, including M.C.'s, engaged, and that now she is ordered to be out of it by Saturday the 3rd. inst.; and that, independently of the ruin it brings on her, by her lost outlay, she neither has, nor can find, another shelter for her own head. I know nothing about it myself, but promised to bring it to your notice. Yours truly,

❊　❊　❊

A woman who had asked the President to use his authority in her behalf at the War Department quoted him: "It's of no use, madam, for me to go. They do things in their own way over there, and I don't amount to pig tracks in the War Department."

❊　❊　❊

To the White House one day came senators who had caucused and decided that the President would do well to reorganize the entire cabinet and set up a new one. "Gentlemen," said Lincoln, "your request for a change of the whole cabinet because I have made one change reminds me of a story." He told of an Illinois farmer pestered by skunks. The farmer's wife was especially wrought up and kept after him to get rid of the varmints. One moonlit night he loaded his shotgun and went out while the wife waited in the house. She heard the shotgun blaze away, and soon her husband came in. "What luck?" she asked. "I hid myself behind the woodpile," said the farmer, "with the shotgun pointed toward the henroost, and before long there appeared not one skunk but *seven*. I took aim, blazed away, killed one and he raised such a fearful smell that I concluded it was best to let the other six go." The senators got no further with their proposal.

THE COMMON PEOPLE

"Common-looking people are the best in the world; that is the reason the Lord makes so many of them."

☼   ☼   ☼

"The people's will, constitutionally expressed, is the ultimate law for all."

October 19, 1864

☼   ☼   ☼

Message to Congress in Special Session
July 4, 1861:

"A right result, at this time, will be worth more to the world than ten times the men and ten times the money. The evidence reaching us from the country leaves no doubt that the material for the work is abundant, and that it needs only the hand of legislation to give it legal sanction, and the hand of the executive to give it practical shape and efficiency. One of the greatest perplexities of the Government is to avoid receiving troops faster than it can provide for them. In a word, the people will save their Government if the Government itself will do its part only indifferently well."

☼   ☼   ☼

From a letter to Brigadier General McClernand
Nov. 10, 1861:

The plain matter-of-fact is, our good people have rushed to the rescue of the government, faster than the government can find arms to put into their hands.

☼   ☼   ☼

Lincoln made himself accessible to the people as often as possible:

"I tell you," he once said, "that I call these receptions my 'public opinion baths'—for I have little time to read the papers and gather public opinion that way; and though they may not be pleasant in all particulars, the effect, as a whole, is renovating and invigorating."

❊   ❊   ❊

July 4, 1861, message to Congress:

"This is essentially a people's contest. On the side of the Union, it is a struggle for maintaining in the world that form and substance of government whose leading object is to elevate the condition of men—to lift artificial weights from all shoulders—to clear the paths of laudable pursuit for all—to afford all an unfettered start, and a fair chance, in the race of life."

❊   ❊   ❊

To law partner William Herndon:

"Billy, don't shoot too high—aim lower and the common people will understand you. They are the ones you want to reach— at least they are the ones you ought to reach. The educated and refined people will understand you anyway. If you aim too high your ideas will go over the heads of the masses and only hit those who need no hitting."

THE CONFEDERATES

An anecdote Lincoln used when he was asked what he would do with Jefferson Davis when the Confederate leader was captured:

"When I was a boy in Indiana, I went to a neighbor's house one morning and found a boy of my own size holding a coon by a string. I asked him what he had and what he was doing. He says, 'It's a coon. Dad cotched six last night, and killed all but this poor little cuss. Dad told me to hold him until he came back, and I'm afraid he's going to kill this one too; and oh, Abe, I do wish he would get away!' 'Well, why don't you let him loose?' 'That wouldn't be right; and if I let him go, Dad would give me hell. But if he would get away himself, it would be all right.'

"Now," said Mr. Lincoln, "if Jeff Davis and those other fellows will only get away, it will be all right. But if we should catch them, and I should let them go, 'Dad would give me hell.'"

DEATH . . . AND TAXES

"I have all my life been a fatalist."

☼   ☼   ☼

"I know I'm in danger, but I'm not going to worry about it."

☼   ☼   ☼

"I long ago made up my mind that if anyone wants to kill me, he will do it. If I wore a shirt of mail, and kept myself surrounded by a bodyguard, it would be all the same. There are a thousand ways of getting at a man if it is desired that he should be killed."

☼   ☼   ☼

He told friends about a dream he had just before the fall of Richmond. In the dream he was wandering through the halls of the White House. He could hear people sobbing, but as he went from room to room, he saw no one.

He kept on until he reached the East Room of the White House: "There I met with a sickening surprise. Before me was a . . . corpse wrapped in funeral vestments. Around it were stationed soldiers who were acting as guards; and there was a throng of people, some gazing mournfully upon the corpse, whose face was covered, others weeping pitifully. 'Who is dead in the White House?' I demanded of one of the soldiers. 'The President,' was his answer; 'he was killed by an assassin.' Then came a loud burst of grief from the crowd, which awoke me from my dream. I slept no more that night."

☼   ☼   ☼

One August night as he was riding on horseback to the Soldiers' Home, he heard a sudden rifle shot and the whistle of a bullet. He gave a humorous account of the incident to his friend Ward Hill Lamon. His horse, "Old Abe," gave a sudden bound, and, as Lincoln told it, "unceremoniously separated me from my eight-dollar plug-hat, with which I parted company without any assent, expressed or implied, upon my part."

❊ ❊ ❊

After the death of his son Willie in 1862:
"He was too good for this earth. It is hard, hard to have him die."

❊ ❊ ❊

He said of the war, "Whichever way it ends, I have the impression I shan't last long after it's over."

❊ ❊ ❊

To Joshua Speed about ten days before his second inauguration: "I ought not to undergo what I so often do. I am very unwell now; my feet and hands of late seem to be always cold, and I ought perhaps to be in bed . . ."
To Mrs. Harriet Beecher Stowe he had made a stronger statement: "I shall never live to see peace; this war is killing me."

❊ ❊ ❊

Letter to William S. Wait
Vandalia, March 2, 1939:

Sir: Your favour of yesterday was handed me by Mr. Dale. In relation to the Revenue law, I think there is something to be feared from the argument you suggest, though I hope the danger is not as great as you apprehend. The passage of a Revenue law at this session, is *right* within itself; and I never despaired of sustaining myself before the people upon any measure that will stand a full investigation. I presume I hardly need to enter into an argument to prove to *you*, that our old revenue system, raising, as it did, all the state revenue from non-resident lands, and those lands' rapid *decreasing*, by passing into the hands of resident owners, while the wants of the Treasury were *increasing* with the increase of population, could not longer continue to answer the purpose of its creation. That proposition is little less than self-evident. The only question is as to sustaining the change before the people. I believe it can be sustained, because it does not increase the tax upon the "many poor" but upon the "wealthy few" by taxing the land that is worth $50 or $100 per acre, in proportion to its value, instead of, as heretofore, no more than that which was worth but $5 per acre. This valuable land, as is well known, belongs, not to the poor, but to the wealthy citizen.

On the other hand, the wealthy can not *justly* complain, because the change is equitable within itself, and also a *sine qua non* to a compliance with the Constitution. If, however, the wealthy should, regardless of the justness of the complaint, as men often [do], when interest is involved in the question, complain of the change, it is still to be remembered, that *they* are not sufficiently numerous to carry the elections.

Very Respectfully,

THE DECLARATION OF INDEPENDENCE

"I have never had a feeling politically that did not spring from the sentiments embodied in the Declaration of Independence."

✿   ✿   ✿

"Little by little but steadily as man's march to the grave, we have been giving up the old for the new faith. Near eighty years ago we began by declaring that all men are created equal; but now from that beginning we have run down to the other declaration that for some men to enslave others is a 'sacred right of self-government.' These principles cannot stand together. They are as opposite as God and Mammon; whoever holds to the one must despise the other."

✿   ✿   ✿

From a speech at Springfield, June 26, 1857:

"I think the authors intended to include *all* men, but they did not intend to declare all men equal *in all respects*. They did not mean to say that all were equal in color, size, intellect, moral development, or social capacity. They defined with tolerable distinctness, in what respects they did consider all men created equal—equal in 'certain inalienable rights, among which are life, liberty, and the pursuit of happiness.' This they said, and this they meant."

✿   ✿   ✿

Independence Hall
February 22, 1861:
Mr. Cuyler:
I am filled with deep emotion at finding myself standing here in the place where were collected together the wisdom, the patriotism, the devotion to principle, from which sprang the

institutions under which we live. You have kindly suggested to me that in my hands is the task of restoring peace to our distracted country. I can say in return, sir, that all the political sentiments I entertain have been drawn, so far as I have been able to draw them, from the sentiments which originated, and were given to the world from this hall in which we stand. . . . I have often pondered over the dangers which were incurred by the men who assembled here and adopted that Declaration of Independence—I have pondered over the toils that were endured by the officers and soldiers of the army, who achieved that independence. I have often inquired of myself, what great principle or idea it was that kept this confederacy so long together. It was not the mere matter of the separation of the colonies from the mother land; but something in that Declaration giving liberty, not alone to the people of this country, but hope to the world for all future time. It was that which gave promise that in due time the weights should be lifted from the shoulders of all men, and that *all* should have an equal chance. This is the sentiment embodied in that Declaration of Independence.

✿　✿　✿

"Now, my friends, can this country be saved upon that basis? If it can, I will consider myself one of the happiest men in the world if I can help to save it. If it can't be saved upon that principle, it will be truly awful. But, if this country cannot be saved without giving up that principle—I was about to say I would rather be assassinated on this spot than to surrender it."

✿　✿　✿

"They [the fathers who issued the Declaration] meant to set up a standard maxim for free society, which should be familiar to all, and revered by all; constantly looked to, constantly labored for, and even though never perfectly attained, constantly approximated, and thereby constantly spreading and deepening its influence, and augmenting the happiness and value of life to all people of all colors everywhere."

✿　✿　✿

17

"And I do think—I repeat, though I said it on a former occasion—that Judge Douglas, and whoever like him teaches that the Negro has no share, humble though it may be, in the Declaration of Independence, in going back to the era of our liberty and independence, and, so far as in him lies, muzzling the cannon that thunders its annual joyous return; that he is *blowing out the moral lights around us*, when he contends that whoever wants slaves has a right to hold them; that he is penetrating, so far as lies in his power, the human soul, and eradicating the light of reason and the love of liberty, when he is in every possible way preparing the public mind, by his vast influence, for making the institution of slavery perpetual and national."

❀   ❀   ❀

Regarding Douglas's defense of the Dred Scott decision:

"Suppose after you read it [the Declaration of Independence] in the old-fashioned way, you read it once more with Judge Douglas's version. It will run thus: 'We hold these truths to be self-evident, that all British subjects who were on this continent eighty-one years ago, were created equal to all British subjects born and *then* residing in Great Britain.' "

❀   ❀   ❀

"Those who would shiver into fragments the Union of these States, tear to tatters its now venerated Constitution, and even bury the last copy of the Bible, rather than slavery should continue a single hour, together with all their more halting sympathizers, have received, and are receiving their just execration; and the name, and opinions, and influence of Mr. Clay, are fully, and, as I trust, effectively and enduringly, arrayed against them. But I would also, if I could, array his name, opinions, and influence against the opposite extreme—against a few but an increasing number of men who, for the sake of perpetuating slavery, are beginning to assail and to ridicule the white man's charter of freedom—the declaration that "all men are created free and equal."

JUDGE DOUGLAS

"Douglas will tell a lie to ten thousand people one day, even though he knows he may have to deny it to five thousand the next day."

✿   ✿   ✿

From a speech on the Kansas-Nebraska Act at Peoria, Illinois:

"The Judge has already informed you that he is to have an hour to reply to me. I doubt not but you have been a little surprised to learn that I have consented to give one of his high reputation and known ability, this advantage of me. Indeed, my consenting to it, though reluctant, was not wholly unselfish; for I suspected if it were understood that the judge was entirely done, you democrats would leave, and not hear me; but by giving him the close, I felt confident you would stay for the fun of hearing him skin me."

Lincoln complained that Douglas was twisting and distorting the issue through a "fantastic arrangement of words, by which a man can prove a horse chestnut to be a chestnut horse."

✿   ✿   ✿

Stephen Douglas and Lincoln had been rivals for twenty years. Douglas had risen to national prominence. He had been a judge of the Illinois Supreme Court, a congressman and a senator, and an outstanding leader of the Democratic party. Lincoln's political career had floundered after his one term in Congress.

"With me, the race of ambition has been a failure—a flat failure. With him it has been one of splendid success. His name fills the nation and is not unknown, even, in foreign lands."

✿   ✿   ✿

"He thought he could approach an argument and at times believed he could make one; but when one denied the settled and plainest facts of history, you could not argue with him: the only thing you could do would be to stop his mouth with a corn cob."

❄   ❄   ❄

To a pretty young woman Abolitionist who told Douglas she didn't like his speech, Lincoln said: "Don't bother, young lady. We'll hang the judge's hide on the fence tomorrow."

❄   ❄   ❄

"I will also add to the remarks I have made, that I have never had the least apprehension that I or my friends would marry Negroes if there was no law to keep them from it. But as Judge Douglas and his friends seem to be in great apprehension that they might, if there were no law to keep them from it, I give him the most solemn pledge that I will to the very last stand by the law of this State, which forbids the marrying of white people with Negroes.

"I will add one further word, which is this, that I do not understand there is any place where an alteration of the social and political relations of the Negro and the white man can be made except in the State Legislature—not in the Congress of the United States—and as I do not really apprehend the approach of any such thing myself, and as Judge Douglas seems to be in constant horror that some such danger is rapidly approaching, I propose as the best means to prevent it that he be kept at home and placed in the State Legislature to fight the measure."

❄   ❄   ❄

First Lincoln-Douglas debate, Lincoln's reply:

"As I have not used up so much of my time as I had supposed, I will dwell a little longer upon one or two of these minor topics upon which the Judge has spoken. He has read from my speech in Springfield, in which I say that 'a house

20

divided against itself cannot stand.' Does the Judge say it *can* stand? I don't know whether he does or not. The Judge does not seem to be attending to me just now, but I would like to know if it is his opinion that a house divided against itself *can stand.* If he does, then there is a question of veracity, not between him and me, but between the Judge and an authority of a somewhat higher character."

※　※　※

"Since Judge Douglas has said to you in his conclusion that he had not time in an hour and a half to answer all I had said in an hour, it follows of course that I will not be able to answer in half an hour all that he said in an hour and a half."

※　※　※

From the fifth Lincoln-Douglas debate:

"That is the real issue. That is the issue that will continue in this country when these poor tongues of Judge Douglas and myself shall be silent. It is the eternal struggle between these two principles—right and wrong—throughout the world. They are the two principles that have stood face to face from the beginning of time; and will ever continue to struggle. The one is the common right of humanity and the other the divine right of kings. It is the same principle in whatever shape it develops itself. It is the same spirit that says, 'You work and toil and earn bread, and I'll eat it.' No matter in what shape it comes, whether from the mouth of a king who seeks to bestride the people of his own nation and live by the fruit of their labor, or from one race of men as an apology for enslaving another race, it is the same tyrannical principle. I was glad to express my gratitude at Quincy, and I re-express it here to Judge Douglas— *that he looks to no end of the institution of slavery.* That will help the people to see where the struggle really is."

21

THE DRAFT

A committee of New Yorkers—William M. Tweed, Orison Blunt, John Fox, and Smith Ely—alleging that the draft on the state was beyond their quota, had been refused access to the War Department records by Stanton. They went to Lincoln, saying New York was getting fifty volunteers daily and a postponement of the draft would enable them to enlist all the men called for. Lincoln said he feared if the draft order were postponed volunteering would cease.

"That," said Lincoln, "is human nature. When you think death is after you, you run. But as soon as death stops, you stop."

* * *

When Lincoln was criticized for jailing a prominent Ohio Democrat who had denounced the draft, he snapped back, "Must I shoot a simple-minded soldier boy who deserts while I must not touch a hair of the wily agitator who induces him to desert?"

* * *

On another occasion, Lincoln was assailed by a Northern governor about his draft policy, who insinuated that he would not carry out the president's orders. Lincoln, however, would not back down and ordered Secretary of War Stanton to go right ahead with the draft:

"The governor is like the boy I saw once at the launching of a ship. When everything was ready, they picked out a boy and sent him under the ship to knock away the trigger and let her go. At the critical moment everything depended on the boy. He had to do the job well by a direct, vigorous blow, and then lie flat and keep still while the ship slid over him. The boy did everything right; but he yelled as if he were being murdered, from the time he got under the keel until he got out. I thought the skin was all scraped off his back; but he wasn't hurt at all. The master of the yard told me that this boy was always chosen for that job, that he did his work well, that he never had been hurt, but that he always squealed in that way. That's just the way with the governor. Make up your minds that he is not hurt, and that he is doing his work right, and pay no attention to his squealing. He only wants to make you understand how hard his task is, and that he is on hand performing it."

✿ ✿ ✿

To James R. Gilmore, regarding the New York draft riots and a recommendation for a special commissioner to expose the instigators of same:

"Well, you see, if I had said no, I should have admitted that I dare not enforce the laws, and consequently have no business to be President of the United States. If I had said yes, and had appointed the judge, I should—as he would have done his duty—have simply touched a match to a barrel of gunpowder. You have heard of sitting on a volcano. We are sitting upon two; one is blazing away already, and the other will blaze away the moment we scrape a little loose dirt from the top of the crater. Better let the dirt alone—at least for the present. One rebellion at a time is about as much as we can conveniently handle."

THE EARLY YEARS

"It is a great piece of folly to attempt to make anything out of my early life. It can all be condensed into a simple sentence, and that sentence you will find in Gray's Elegy—'the short and simple annals of the poor.' That's my life, and that's all you or anyone else can make out of it."

☼   ☼   ☼

Lincoln mocked his own part in the Black Hawk War:

"Among the rules and regulations, no man is to wear more than five pounds of cod-fish or epaulets, or more than thirty yards of bologna sausage for a sash, and no two men are to dress alike, and if any two should dress alike, the one that dresses most alike is to be fined."

☼   ☼   ☼

From an early political speech, Pappsville, Illinois, July 1832:

"Fellow citizens, I presume you all know who I am. I am humble Abraham Lincoln. I have been solicited by many friends to become a candidate for the legislature. My politics are short and sweet, like the old woman's dance. I am in favor of a national bank. I am in favor of the internal-improvements system and a high protective tariff. These are my sentiments and political principles. If elected, I shall be thankful; if not, it will be all the same."

☼   ☼   ☼

Later Lincoln joked about his three-month stint as a military man in the Black Hawk War, telling how he survived "a good many bloody battles with mosquitoes."

☼   ☼   ☼

Address before Young Men's Lyceum of Springfield, Illinois, January 27, 1838:

"At what point then is the approach of danger to be expected? I answer, if it ever reach us, it must spring up amongst us. It cannot come from abroad. If destruction be our lot, we must ourselves be its author and finisher. As a nation of freemen, we must live through all time, or die by suicide."

✿   ✿   ✿

A mover came by, heading west in a covered wagon. He sold Lincoln a barrel. Lincoln afterward explained, "I did not want it, but to oblige him I bought it, and paid him half a dollar for it." Later, emptying rubbish out of the barrel, he found books, and at the bottom, Blackstone's *Commentaries on the Laws of England*. By a streak of luck, he was now owner of the one famous book that any young man studying law had to read first.

✿   ✿   ✿

Upon his arrival in Springfield in 1837, Lincoln pulled in his horse at the general store of Joshua Speed. He asked the price of bedclothes for a single bedstead, which Speed figured at $17.00. "Cheap as it is, I have not the money to pay," he told Speed. "But if you will credit me until Christmas, and my experiment as a lawyer here is a success, I will pay you then. If I fail in that I will probably never pay you at all." Speed offered to share his own big double bed upstairs over the store. Lincoln took his saddlebags upstairs, came down with his face lit up and said, "Well, Speed, I'm moved."

✿   ✿   ✿

A story arose that a pompous and punctilious challenger had come to him and told him that honor would have to be satisfied by mortal and bloody combat in the medieval manner, saying, "As the challenged party you will have the choice of weapons—

what will your weapons be?" Lincoln's reply was, "How about cow-dung at five paces?"

* * *

He was sued for ten dollars owing on his horse; a friend let him have the ten dollars; the horse was saved. He was sued again, and his horse, saddle, bridle, and surveying instruments were taken. James Short, a Sand Ridge farmer, heard about it. He liked Lincoln as a serious student, a pleasant joker, and a swift cornhusker. He had told people, when Lincoln worked for him, "He husks two loads of corn to my one."

Short went to the auction, bought the horse and outfit for $125.00, and gave them back to Lincoln. Lincoln had stayed away from the auction, too sad to show up. And when Short came along with his horse, saddle, bridle, compass, and all, it hit him as another surprise in his life.

* * *

On being shown rails he may have split years earlier.

"What kind of timber are they?" he asked, getting into the spirit of the fun. "Honey locust and black walnut." "Well, that is lasting timber. It may be that I split these rails. Well, boys, I can only say that I have split a great many better-looking ones."

* * *

Farewell address at Springfield, Illinois
February 11, 1861:

"My Friends:
"No one, not in my situation, can appreciate my feeling of sadness at this parting. To this place, and the kindness of these people, I owe everything. Here I have lived a quarter of a century, and have passed from a young to an old man. Here my children have been born, and one is buried. I now leave, not knowing when or whether ever I may return, with a task before

me greater than that which rested upon Washington. Without the assistance of that Divine Being who ever attended him, I cannot succeed. With that assistance, I cannot fail. Trusting in Him who can go with me, and remain with you, and be every-where for good, let us confidently hope that all will yet be well. To His care commending you, as I hope in your prayers you will commend me, I bid you an affectionate farewell."

✿ ✿ ✿

His run for Congress was against Peter Cartwright, an old-fashioned circuit rider, famous as an evangelist and exhorter, and a Jackson Democrat.

In spite of warnings, he went to a religious meeting where Cartwright was to preach. In due time Cartwright said, "All who desire to lead a new life, to give their hearts to God, and go to heaven, will stand," and a sprinkling of men, women, and children stood up. Then the preacher exhorted, "All who do not wish to go to hell will stand." All stood up—except Lincoln. Then, said Cartwright in his gravest voice, "I observe that many responded to the first invitation to give their hearts to God and go to heaven. And I further observe that all of you save one indicated that you did not desire to go to hell. The sole excep-tion is Mr. Lincoln, who did not respond to either invitation. May I inquire of you, Mr. Lincoln, where you are going?"

Lincoln slowly rose and spoke. "I came here as a respectful listener. I did not know that I was to be singled out by Brother Cartwright. I believe in treating religious matters with due solemnity. I admit that the questions propounded by Brother Cartwright are of great importance. I did not feel called upon to answer as the rest did. Brother Cartwright asks me directly where I am going. I desire to reply with equal directness: I am going to Congress."

EDUCATION

"The things I want to know are in books; my best friend is the man who'll git me a book I ain't read."

❋   ❋   ❋

"My father grew up, literally without education. He moved from Kentucky to what is now Spencer county, Indiana, in my eighth year. It was a wild region, with many bears and other wild animals still in the woods. There were some schools, so called; but no qualification was ever required of a teacher, beyond 'readin, writin, and cipherin, to the Rule of Three.' If a straggler, supposed to understand Latin, happened to sojourn in the neighborhood, he was looked upon as a wizard."

❋   ❋   ❋

Lincoln said later that all his schooling together "did not amount to one year." Some fragments of his schoolwork still survive, including a verse he wrote in his homemade arithmetic book:
"Abraham Lincoln/his hand and pen/he will be good but/god knows When."

❋   ❋   ❋

From lecture before the Springfield Library Association, February 22, 1860:

"Writing, the art of communicating thoughts to the mind through the eye, is the great invention of the world . . . enabling us to converse with the dead, the absent, and the unborn, at all distances of time and space."

❋   ❋   ❋

Lincoln had a great reverence for learning.

"This is not because I am not an educated man. I feel the need of reading. It is a loss to a man not to have grown up among books."

✿ ✿ ✿

Address to the Young Men's Lyceum of Springfield, Illinois:

"Upon the subject of education, not presuming to dictate any plan or system respecting it, I can only say that I view it as the most important subject which we as a people can be engaged in. That every man may receive, at least, a moderate education, and thereby be enabled to read the histories of his own and other countries, by which he may duly appreciate the value of our free institutions, appears to be an object of vital importance, even on this account alone, to say nothing of the advantages and satisfaction to be derived from all being able to read the scriptures and other words, both of a religious and moral nature, for themselves. For my part, I desire to see the time when education, and by its means, morality, sobriety, enterprise and industry, shall become much more general than at present, and should be gratified to have it in my power to contribute something to the advancement of any measure which might have a tendency to accelerate the happy period."

THE EMANCIPATION PROCLAMATION

"If my name ever goes into history, it will be for this act."

         ✿ ✿ ✿

On September 24, 1862, a Monday morning, a preliminary Emancipation Proclamation was published. The President held that to have issued it six months earlier would have been too soon. What he called "public sentiment" would not have stood for it. "A man watches his pear-tree day after day, impatient for the ripening of the fruit. Let him attempt to *force* the process and he may spoil both fruit and tree. But let him patiently *wait*, and the ripe pear at length falls into his lap. . . . I have done what no man could have helped doing, standing in my place."

         ✿ ✿ ✿

The Emancipation Proclamation struck at property valued on tax books at nearly $3,000,000.

To those who shrank in horror from the act, Lincoln at a later time made his argument:

"You dislike the Emancipation Proclamation, and perhaps would have it retracted. You say it is unconstitutional. I think differently. I think the Constitution invests its commander-in-chief with the law of war in time of war. The most that can be said—if so much—is that slaves are property. Is there—has there ever been—any question that by the law of war, property, both of enemies and friends, may be taken when needed? And is it not needed whenever taking it helps us or hurts the enemy? Armies, the world over, destroy enemies' property when they cannot use it; and even destroy their own to keep it from the enemy. Civilized belligerents do all in their power to

30

help themselves or hurt the enemy, except a few things regarded as barbarous or cruel."

✿ ✿ ✿

When critics demanded that he change his emancipation policy:

"I am a slow walker, but I never walk backward."

FAMILY—HIS CHILDREN

"It is my pleasure that my children are free, happy and unrestrained by parental tyranny. Love is the chain whereby to bind a child to its parents."

✿　✿　✿

From a letter to Joshua Speed, 1845:

We have another boy, born the 10th of March last. He is very much such a child as Bob was at his age—rather of a longer order. . . . Bob is "short and low," and I expect, always will be. He talks very plainly—almost as plainly as anybody. He is quite smart enough. I some times fear he is one of the little rare-ripe sort, that are smarter at about five than ever after. He has a great deal of that sort of mischief that is the offspring of much animal spirits. Since I began this letter a messenger came to tell me Bob was lost; but by the time I reached the house, his mother had found him, and had him whipped, and, by now, very likely he is run away again.

✿　✿　✿

Once he lugged away the howling Willie and Tad, and a neighbor asked, "Why, Mr. Lincoln, what's the matter?" The answer: "Just what's the matter with the whole world. I've got three walnuts and each wants two."

✿　✿　✿

Lincoln took Tad's dislike of study calmly.

"Let him run. There's time enough yet for him to learn his letters and get poky. Bob was just such a little rascal, and now he is a very decent boy."

September 8, 1864
Mrs. A. Lincoln
Manchester, Vermont

All well, including Tad's pony and the goats. Mrs. Col. Dimmick died night before last. Bob left Sunday afternoon. Said he did not know whether he should see you.

✽ ✽ ✽

During the war, Lincoln sometimes issued a proclamation for a national fast. When Tad found out the meaning of such a day, he was dismayed. He promptly established a food cache under the seat of a coach in the carriage house, and stocked it from the White House kitchen. The President laughed over the incident:

"If he grows to be a man, Tad will be what the women all dote on—a good provider."

✽ ✽ ✽

In the Illinois State Historical Library at Springfield a miniature brass cannon is preserved with this note:

"Capt. Dahlgren may let 'Tad' have a little gun that he cannot hurt himself with.
A. Lincoln"

✽ ✽ ✽

When Robert told his father he wished to study law at Harvard, Lincoln replied:

"If you do, you should learn more than I ever did, but you will never have so good a time."

✽ ✽ ✽

On his journey to Washington, a gripsack held his copy of the inaugural address he hoped to deliver on March 4. In Harrisburg he trusted it to his son Robert, who, when asked for it, said he believed he had given it to a waiter. Lincoln spoke witheringly to his boy.

To Lamon he spoke confidentially: "I guess I have lost my certificate of moral character, written by myself. Bob has lost my gripsack containing my inaugural address. I want you to help me find it. I feel a good deal as the old member of the Methodist church did when he lost his wife at the camp meeting, and went up to an old elder of the church and asked him if he could tell him whereabouts in hell his wife was. In fact, I am in a worse fix than my Methodist friend, for if it were nothing but a wife missing, mine would be sure to pop up serenely somewhere. That address may be a loss to more than one husband in this country, but I shall be the greatest sufferer."

In the hotel baggage room they looked over a pile of bags, valises, and satchels. Eventually they found the gripsack with the missing document. Lincoln took it in charge, said it wouldn't leave his own hands again, and told the story of a man who had saved $1,500. The bank keeping the money failed and the man got $150 as his share. This he put into another bank that failed and he got $15 as his share. As he looked at what was left of his savings, he said, "Now, darn you, I've got you reduced to portable shape, so I'll put you in my pocket."

FAMILY—HIS WIFE

In a letter shortly after his marriage:

Nothing new here, except my marrying, which, to me, is a matter of profound wonder.

❖   ❖   ❖

In a letter to his wife:

Suppose you do not prefix the "Hon" to the address on your letters to me any more. I like the letters very much but I would rather they should not have that upon them.

❖   ❖   ❖

From another letter to his wife:

Are you entirely free from headache? That is good—good considering it is the first spring you have been free from it since we were acquainted. . . . I am afraid you will get so well, and fat, and young, as to be wanting to marry again.

❖   ❖   ❖

After a storm of anger:

"It does her lots of good and it doesn't hurt me a bit."

❖   ❖   ❖

After his nomination for President at the Chicago Convention:

"There's a little woman down at our house would like to hear this. I'll go down and tell her."

❖   ❖   ❖

In January 1861, after election, Lincoln received lots of mail enclosing gifts, including an elegant hat. Trying it on playfully, he remarked with a smile:

"Well, wife, there is one thing likely to come out of this scrape, anyhow. We are going to have some *new clothes*."

❖ ❖ ❖

Low-necked dresses were controversial at the time. Mrs. Lincoln probably considered Lincoln's attitude behind the times. Just before a reception, he viewed her in a gown with a long train: "Whew!" he remarked teasingly. "Our cat has a long tail to-night." Then, in the gentle paternal manner he used in offering advice, he continued, "Mother, it is my opinion if some of that tail was nearer the head, it would be in better style."

❖ ❖ ❖

Regarding gossip about his wife's interest in politics:

"Tell the gentlemen not to be alarmed, for I myself manage all important matters. In little things I have got along through life by letting my wife run her end of the machine pretty much in her own way."

❖ ❖ ❖

Mrs. Lincoln disliked Grant and advised her husband to remove him.

"Well, Mother, supposing that we give you command of the army. No doubt you would do much better than any general that has been tried."

❖ ❖ ❖

August 8, 1863
My dear Wife:

All as well as usual, and no particular trouble any way. I put the money into the Treasury at five per cent, with the privilege of withdrawing it any time upon thirty days' notice. I suppose you are glad to learn this. Tell dear Tad, poor "Nanny Goat," is lost; and Mrs. Cuthbert & I are in distress about it. The day you left Nanny was found resting herself, and chewing her little cud, on the middle of Tad's bed. But now she's gone! The gardener kept complaining that she destroyed the flowers, till it was concluded to bring her down to the White House. This was done, and the second day she had disappeared, and has not been heard of since. This is the last we know of poor "Nanny."

✿　✿　✿

April 28, 1864

Mrs. A. Lincoln
Metropolitan Hotel, New York

The draft will go to you. Tell Tad the goats and father are very well—especially the goats.

FAMILY—HIS WIFE'S

Mary Todd, Lincoln's wife, came from a high-toned family. He was once asked whether the Todds spelled their name with one or two *d's*.

"One *d* is enough for God," Lincoln said. "But the Todds need two."

✿   ✿   ✿

While on the judicial circuit with John Todd Stuart and other lawyers, they stopped at an inn. The landlady remarked at how well Stuart looked, but that Lincoln looked weak.

"Nothing out of the common, ma'am," he replied, "but did you ever see Stuart's wife? or did you ever see mine? I just tell you whoever married into the Todd family gets the worst of it."

✿   ✿   ✿

When "Little Sister" Emilie gave a provoking man just the answer he deserved, Lincoln chuckled: "The child has a tongue like the rest of the Todds."

✿   ✿   ✿

Divided loyalties complicated relations between Tad and his cousin Katherine Helm. The children were seated on a rug in front of the fire one evening, Tad entertaining his guest by showing photographs. Holding up one of his father, he said with great pride, "This is the President." Katherine shook her head in emphatic denial: "No, that is not the President, Mr. Davis is President." Tad was outraged and shouted, "Hurrah for Abe Lincoln." Little Katherine had the same amount of Todd blood as Tad, so she promptly yelled, "Hurrah for Jeff Davis." As usual, Tad appealed to his father, who, with twinkling eyes, drew the two belligerents into his lap, one on each knee, and exercised his statesmanship, saying: "Well, Tad, you know who is your President, and I am your little cousin's Uncle Lincoln."

August 8, 1864
Major General Burbridge
Lexington, Ky.

Last December Mrs. Emily T. Helm, half-sister of Mrs. Lincoln and widow of the rebel general Ben. Hardin Helm, stopped here on her way from Georgia to Kentucky, and I gave her a paper, as I remember, to protect her against the mere fact of her being Gen. Helm's widow. I hear a rumor today that you recently sought to arrest her, but was prevented by her presenting the paper from me. I do not intend to protect her against the consequences of disloyal words or acts, spoken or done by her since her return to Kentucky, and if the paper given her by me can be construed to give her protection for such words or acts, it is hereby revoked *pro tanto*. Deal with her for current conduct, just as you would with *any other*.

THE FUTURE

To his wife:

We must both be more cheerful in the future. Between the war and the loss of our darling Willie, we have been very miserable.

❖ ❖ ❖

To Noah Brooks:

When we leave this place [the White House], we shall have enough, I think, to take care of us old people. The boys must look out for themselves. I guess Mother will be satisfied with six months or so in Europe. After that, I should really like to go to California and take a look at the Pacific coast.

❖ ❖ ❖

"If we get through this war, and I live, this Indian system shall be reformed."

THE GENERALS

"I will hold McClellan's horse, if he will only bring us success."

❖   ❖   ❖

While McClellan visited his family in Philadelphia, Jeb Stuart led his gray horsemen across the Potomac and up into Chambersburg, Pennsylvania, where he destroyed a machine shop, took 500 horses and Federal uniforms, and all the shoes and clothing in the stores, paying for them with Confederate money and camping his men in the streets. Riding back to join Lee, Stuart rode around McClellan's army for the second time that year.

Lincoln, on the deck of the ship *Martha Washington*, returning from a troop review at Alexandria, was asked, "What about McClellan?" Lincoln drew a ring on the deck and said, "When I was a boy we used to play a game, three times round and out. Stuart has been round him twice. If he goes around him once more, gentlemen, McClellan will be out!"

❖   ❖   ❖

To George B. McClellan
October 24, 1862:

Majr. Genl. McClellan
I have just read your despatch about sore tongued and fatigued horses. Will you pardon me for asking what the horses of your army have done since the battle of Antietam that fatigue anything?

❖   ❖   ❖

"McClellan has got the slows."

❖   ❖   ❖

In a letter to General McClellan, Lincoln used his wit to express his feelings concerning the lack of success of the Union armies.

41

My Dear McClellan:

If you don't want to use the army I should like to borrow it for a while.

Yours respectfully,

A. Lincoln

✿   ✿   ✿

Lincoln remarked to Lamon: "I suppose our victory at Antietam will condone my offence in reappointing McClellan. If the battle had gone against us, poor McClellan and I, too, would be in a bad row of stumps."

✿   ✿   ✿

While McClellan rested his troops a visitor at the White House casually asked Lincoln what number of men he supposed the "rebels" had in the field. And as *Leslie's Weekly* published the reply, he said, "1,200,000 according to the best authority." The visitor cried "My God!" "Yes, sir," went on the President, "1,200,000—no doubt of it. You see, all our generals, when they get whipped, say the enemy outnumbers them from three to five to one, and I must believe them. We have 400,000 men in the field, and three times four makes twelve. Don't you see it?"

✿   ✿   ✿

"It's the same thing with the Army. It doesn't seem worthwhile to secure divorces and then marry the Army and McClellan to others, for they won't get along any better than they do now, and there'll only be a new set of heartaches started.

"I think we'd better wait; perhaps a real fighting general will come along some of these days, and then we'll all be happy. If you go to mixing in a mix-up, you only make the muddle worse."

✿   ✿   ✿

On General Frémont:

"He is losing the confidence of men near him, whose support

any man in his position must have to be successful. His cardinal mistake is that he isolates himself, and allows nobody to see him; and by which he does not know what is going on in the very matter he is dealing with."

❀ ❀ ❀

To Lorenzo Thomas:

July 8, 1863
Gen. Thomas

Your despatch of this morning to the Sec. of War is before me. The forces you speak of, will be of no imagineable service, if they can not go forward with a little more expedition. Lee is now passing the Potomac faster than the forces you mention are passing Carlyle. Forces now beyond Carlyle, to be joined by regiments still at Harrisburg, and the united force again to join Pierce somewhere, and the whole to move down the Cumberland Valley, will, in my unprofessional opinion, be quite as likely to capture the Man-in-the-Moon, as any part of Lee's Army.

❀ ❀ ❀

Once when results were slow from armies in the field, Lincoln (according to Alexander McClure) had this comment:

"Some of my generals are so slow that molasses in the coldest days of winter is a race horse compared to them. They're brave enough, but somehow or other, they get fastened in a fence corner, and can't figure their way out."

❀ ❀ ❀

"Wright telegraphs that he thinks the enemy are all across the Potomac but that he has halted and sent out an infantry reconnaissance, for fear he might come across the rebels and catch some of them."

❀ ❀ ❀

To Major General Hooker
January 26, 1863:

I have placed you at the head of the Army of the Potomac. Of course, I have done this upon what appears to me to be sufficient reasons. And yet I think it best for you to know that there are some things in regard to which I am not quite satisfied with you. I believe you to be a brave and skillful soldier, which, of course, I like. I also believe you do not mix politics with your profession, in which you are right. You have confidence in yourself, which is a valuable, if not an indispensable quality. You are ambitious, which, within reasonable bounds, does good rather than harm. But I think that during Gen. Burnside's command of the Army you have taken counsel of your ambition, and thwarted him as much as you could, in which you did a great wrong to the country, and to a most meritorius and honorable brother officer. I have heard, in such a way as to believe it, of your recently saying that both the Army and the Government needed a Dictator. Of course it was not *for* this, but in spite of it, that I have given you the command. Only those generals who gain successes, can set up dictators. What I now ask of you is military success, and I will risk the dictatorship.

❀   ❀   ❀

In the matter of giving Lew Wallace of Indiana an army command, Senator Lane of Indiana called on Lincoln, who remarked to a later caller, "Halleck wants to kick Wallace out, and Lane wants me to kick Halleck out."

"Well, I'll tell you how to fix it to the satisfaction of both parties."

"How is that?"

"Why kick 'em both out."

"No, that won't do. I think Halleck is a good man. He may not be, of course; I don't know much about such things. I may be a judge of good lawyers, but I don't know much about generals. Those who ought to know say he is good."

❀   ❀   ❀

44

A senator, on learning from Lincoln that Halleck had nega-
tived proposed military changes, asked the President why he
didn't get Halleck out of the way. "Well—the fact is—the man
who has no friends—should be taken care of."

✿ ✿ ✿

After Gettysburg, when news of the victory reached Lincoln,
he ordered Meade to go after Lee and destroy his army once
and for all: "Do not let the enemy escape."

But Meade hesitated, allowing Lee to move his retreating
troops safely across the Potomac. "We had them within our
grasp. We had only to stretch forth our hands and they were
ours. What can I do with such generals as we have. Who among
them is any better than Meade?"

✿ ✿ ✿

Uneasy about Meade's phrase as to "driving the invader from
our soil," Lincoln said to his secretary, John Hay:

"Will our generals never get that idea out of their heads? The
whole country is our soil."

✿ ✿ ✿

"If General Meade can now attack him [Lee] on a field no
worse than equal for us," said Lincoln, "and will do so with all
the skill and courage, which he, his officers, and men possess,
the honor will be his if he succeeds, and the blame may be
mine if he fails."

✿ ✿ ✿

In Virginia Meade and Lee came to no grapple. According to
William A. Croffut of the *New York Tribune*, when Lincoln and
Meade met after the battle of Gettysburg, Lincoln said: "Do
you know, general, what your attitude toward Lee after the Battle of Gettysburg reminded me of?"

"No, Mr. President, what was it?"

45

"I'll be hanged if I could think of anything but an old woman trying to shoo her geese across the creek."

❖ ❖ ❖

Sep. 26, 1864

Major General Rosecrans:
One cannot always safely disregard a report, even which one may not believe. I have a report that you incline to deny the soldiers the right of attending the election in Missouri, on the assumed ground that they will get drunk and make disturbance. Last year I sent Gen. Schofield a letter of instruction, dated October 1, 1863, which I suppose you will find on the files of the department, and which contains, among other things, the following:
"At elections see that those and only those, are allowed to vote, who are entitled to do so by the laws of Missouri, including as of those laws, the restrictions laid by the Missouri convention upon those who may have participated in the rebellion."
This I thought right then, and think right now; and I may add I do not remember that either party complained after the election, of Gen. Schofield's action under it. Wherever the law allows soldiers to vote, their officers must also allow it. Please write me on this subject. Yours truly,

❖ ❖ ❖

In the many combustible situations where Rosecrans had to make decisions, Lincoln believed Old Rosy had done not so bad. "So far you have got along in the Department of the Missouri rather better than I dared to hope, and I congratulate you and myself upon it."

❖ ❖ ❖

April 7, 1865
Lieut Gen. Grant:
Gen. Sheridan says "If the thing is pressed I think that Lee will surrender." Let the *thing* be pressed."

❖ ❖ ❖

46

The greeting given Sheridan was remembered. The President ended his long handshake with the short general. "General Sheridan, when this peculiar war began I thought a cavalryman should be at least six feet four high, but I have changed my mind—five feet four will do in a pinch."

*　　*　　*

Dec. 26, 1864

My dear General Sherman,

Many, many thanks for your Christmas gift—the capture of Savannah.

When you were about leaving Atlanta for the Atlantic coast, I was anxious, if not fearful; but feeling that you were the better judge, and remembering that "nothing risked, nothing gained" I did not interfere. Now, the undertaking being a success, the honor is all yours; for I believe none of us went farther than to acquiesce. And, taking the work of Gen. Thomas into the count, as it should be taken, it is indeed a great success. Not only does it afford the obvious and immediate military advantages; but, in showing to the world that your army could be divided, putting the stronger part to an important new service, and yet leaving enough to vanquish the old opposing force of the whole—Hood's army—it brings those who sat in darkness, to see a great light. But what next? I suppose it will be safer if I leave Gen. Grant and yourself to decide.

Please make my grateful acknowledgments to your whole army, officers and men. Yours very truly

*　　*　　*

Lincoln commented to one of Grant's staff that once he "gets possession of a place, he holds on to it as if he had inherited it."

*　　*　　*

August 17, 1864
Lieut. Gen. Grant
City Point, Va.

I have seen your despatch expressing your unwillingness to break your hold where you are. Neither am I willing. Hold on with a bull-dog grip, and chew and choke, as much as possible.

❉ ❉ ❉

A member of Congress asked Lincoln what Grant was doing (circa 1864).

"I can't tell much about it. You see, Grant has gone to the Wilderness, crawled in, drawn up the ladder, and pulled in the hole after him, and I guess we'll have to wait till he comes out before we know just what he's up to."

❉ ❉ ❉

"If I had done as my Washington friends, who fight battles with their tongues at a safe distance from the enemy, would have had me do, Grant, who proved himself so great a captain, would never have been heard of again."

(1865)

❉ ❉ ❉

James R. Gilmore, calling on Lincoln in late March, believed he saw a load of care lifted off the President by the prospect of Grant's taking control of army operations and that the President was looking better. The reply was: "Oh, yes! I feel better, for now I'm like the man who was blown up on a steamboat and said, on coming down, 'It makes no difference to me—I'm only a passenger.' "

Gilmore asked Lincoln if he was not putting too much military control in Grant's hands. Lincoln said, "Do you hire a man to do your work and then do it yourself?"

※　※　※

Lincoln adopted a set form to meet a certain question, and according to the *Chicago Journal* the dialogue ran:

Visitor: When will the army move?
Lincoln: Ask General Grant.
Visitor: General Grant will not tell me.
Lincoln: Neither will he tell me.

※　※　※

"Grant is the first general I have had. You know how it has been with all the rest. They wanted me to be the general. I am glad to find a man who can go ahead without me."

※　※　※

To one White House caller Lincoln gave his metaphor of the major strategy of recent weeks (toward the end of the war).

"Grant has the bear by the hind leg while Sherman takes off the hide."

※　※　※

A few weeks after Grant captured Vicksburg, Lincoln sent the victorious general a personal letter of commendation:

"I do not remember that you and I ever met personally. I write this now as a grateful acknowledgment for the almost inestimable service you have done the country. I wish to say a word further. When you first reached the vicinity of Vicksburg . . . I never had any faith, except a general hope that you knew better than I that the expedition could succeed . . . I feared it was a mistake. I now wish to make the personal acknowledgment that you were right, and I was wrong."

GETTYSBURG

"It is what I would call a short, short speech."
                                        (About the Gettysburg address)

❊   ❊   ❊

The evening he arrived at Gettysburg, a crowd gathered and asked him to speak:

"I appear before you, fellow citizens, merely to thank you for this compliment. The inference is a very fair one that you would hear me, for a little while at least, were I to commence to make a speech. I do not appear before you for the purpose of doing so, and for several substantial reasons. The most substantial of these is that I have no speech to make. In my position it is somewhat important that I should not say foolish things. It very often happens that the only way to help it is to say nothing at all. Believing that is my present condition this evening, I must beg of you to excuse me from addressing you further."

❊   ❊   ❊

THE GETTYSBURG ADDRESS

Four score and seven years ago our fathers brought forth on this continent, a new nation, conceived in Liberty, and dedicated to the proposition that all men are created equal.

Now we are engaged in a great civil war, testing whether that nation, or any nation so conceived and so dedicated can long endure. We are met on a great battlefield of that war. We have come to dedicate a portion of that field, as a final resting place for those who here gave their lives that that nation might live. It is altogether fitting and proper that we should do this.

But, in a larger sense, we can not dedicate—we can not consecrate—we can not hallow—this ground. The brave men, living and dead, who struggled here, have consecrated it, far above our poor power to add or detract. The world will little note, nor long remember what we say here, but it can never forget what they did here. It is for us the living, rather, to be dedicated here to the unfinished work which they who fought here have thus far so nobly advanced. It is rather for us to be here dedicated to the great task remaining before us—that from these honored dead we take increased devotion to that cause for which they gave the last full measure of devotion—that we here highly resolve that these dead shall not have died in vain—that this nation, under God, shall have a new birth of freedom—and that government of the people, by the people, for the people, shall not perish from the earth.

November 19, 1863

✿ ✿ ✿

Nov. 20, 1863
Hon. Edward Everett

My dear Sir:
Your kind note of today is received. In our respective parts yesterday, you could not have been excused to make a short address, nor I a long one. I am pleased to know that, in your judgment, the little I did say was not entirely a failure. Of course I knew Mr. Everett would not fail; and yet, while the whole discourse was eminently satisfactory, and will be of great value, there were passages in it which transcended my expectation. The point made against the theory of the general government being only an agency, whose principals are the states, was new to me, and, as I think, is one of the best arguments for the national supremacy. The tribute to our noble women for their angel-ministering to the suffering soldiers, surpasses, in its way, as do the subjects of it, whatever has gone before.
Our sick boy, for whom you kindly inquire, we hope is past the worst. Your obt. Servt.

GOVERNMENT

"Understanding the spirit of our institutions is to aim at the elevation of men; I am opposed to whatever tends to degrade them."

      ✿   ✿   ✿

"The government has a difficult duty to perform. At the very best, it will by turns do both too little and too much. It can properly have no motive of revenge, no purpose to punish merely for punishment's sake. While we must, by all available means, prevent the overthrow of the government, we should avoid planting and cultivating too many thorns in the bosom of society."

      ✿   ✿   ✿

When a delegation invaded his office making excited demands:
"Gentlemen, suppose all the property you were worth was in gold and this you had placed in the hands of [one man] to carry across the Niagara River on a rope. Would you shake the cable and keep shouting at him: 'Stand up a little straighter, stoop a little more, go a little faster, go a little slower, lean a little more to the south?' No, you would hold your breath, as well as your tongue, and keep your hands off until he got safely over.
"The Government is carrying an enormous weight. Untold treasure is in their hands. Don't badger them. Keep silence and we will get you safely across."

      ✿   ✿   ✿

"Any people anywhere, being inclined and having the power, have the *right* to rise up, and shake off the existing government, and form a new one that suits them better. This is a most valuable, a most sacred right—a right, which we hope and believe, is to liberate the world. Nor is this right confined to cases in which the whole people of an existing government may choose to exercise it. Any portion of such people that *can, may* revolutionize, and make their own, of so much of the territory as they inhabit. More than this, a *majority* of any portion of such people may revolutionize, putting down a *minority*, intermingled with, or near about them, who may oppose their movement. Such minority was precisely the case of the tories of our own revolution. It is a quality of revolutions not to go by *old* lines, or *old* laws; but to break up both, and make new ones."

(1848)

✿   ✿   ✿

Fragment on Government
(circa 1854):

The legitimate object of government, is to do for a community of people, whatever they need to have done, but can not do, *at all*, or can not, *so well do*, for themselves—in their separate and individual capacities.

In all that the people can individually do as well for themselves, government ought not to interfere.

The desirable things which the individuals of a people can not do, or can not well do, for themselves, fall into two classes: those which have relation to *wrongs*, and those which have not. Each of these branch off into an infinite variety of subdivisions.

The first—that in relation to wrongs—embraces all crimes, misdemeanors, and non-performance of contracts. The other embraces all which, in its nature, and without wrong, requires combined action, as public roads and highways, public schools, charities, pauperism, orphanage, estates of the deceased, and the machinery of government itself.

From this it appears that if all men were just, there still would be *some*, though not *so much*, need of government.

✿   ✿   ✿

Most governments have been based, practically, on the denial of equal rights of men, as I have, in part, stated them; ours

53

began by affirming those rights. They said, some men are too ignorant and vicious to share in government. Possibly so, said we; and, by your system, you would always keep them ignorant, and vicious. We proposed to give all a chance; and we expected the weak to grow stronger, the ignorant, wiser; and all better, and happier together.

We made the experiment; and the fruit is before us. Look at it—think of it. Look at it, in its aggregate grandeur, of extent of country, and numbers of population—ship, and steamboat, and rail.

(1854)

✿   ✿   ✿

Address to the Young Men's Lyceum of Springfield, Illinois:

"I know the American People are *much* attached to their Government; I know they would suffer *much* for its sake; I know they would endure evils long and patiently, before they would ever think of exchanging it for another. Yet, notwithstanding all this, if the laws be continually despised and disregarded, if their rights to be secure in their persons and property are held by no better tenure than the caprice of a mob, the alienation of their affections from the Government is the natural consequence; and to that, sooner or later, it must come."

✿   ✿   ✿

To John Hay, Lincoln's secretary:

For my own part, I consider the first necessity that is upon us, is of proving that popular government is not an absurdity. We must settle this question now,—whether in a free government the minority have the right to break it up whenever they choose. If we fail, it will go far to prove the incapability of the people to govern themselves. There may be one consideration used in stay of such final judgment, but that is not for us to use in advance. That is, that there exists in our case an instance of a

vast and far-reaching disturbing element which the history of
no other free nation will probably ever present. That, however,
is not for us to say at present. Taking the government as we
found it, we will see if the majority can preserve it.

❉   ❉   ❉

On his desk lay a report having much useless language, the
work of a congressional committee regarding a newly devised
gun. "I should want a new lease of life to read this through,"
groaned the President. "Why can't an investigating committee
show a grain of common sense? If I send a man to buy a horse
for me, I expect him to tell me that horse's points—not how
many hairs he has in his tail."

HIMSELF

"If any personal description of me is thought desirable, it may be said, I am, in height, six feet, four inches, nearly; lean in flesh, weighing, on average, one hundred and eighty pounds; dark complexion, with coarse black hair and gray eyes—no other marks or brands recollected."

✿ ✿ ✿

From a letter to the editor of *Sangamo Journal,* June 13, 1836:

Every man is said to have his peculiar ambition. . . . I have no other so great as that of being truly esteemed of my fellow men, by rendering myself worthy of their esteem.

✿ ✿ ✿

When a rival called him "two-faced" during a political debate, Lincoln replied: "I leave it to my audience. If I had another face, do you think I'd wear this one?"

✿ ✿ ✿

General Egbert L. Viele, military governor of Norfolk, spent many hours with Lincoln on a steamboat. Lincoln said to Viele one morning: "If I have one vice, and I can call it nothing else, it is not to be able to say 'No.' Thank God for not making me a woman, but if He had, I suppose He would have made me just as ugly as He did, and no one would ever have tempted me."

✿ ✿ ✿

Washington, Jan. 5, 1849
Mr. C.U. Schlater:

Dear Sir:
Your note, requesting my "signature with a sentiment" was received, and should have been answered long since, but that it

was mislaid. I am not a very sentimental man; and the best sentiment I can think of is, that if you collect the signatures of all persons who are no less distinguished than I, you will have a very undistinguishing mass of names.

Very respectfully,

❊ ❊ ❊

"I shall never be old enough to speak without embarrassment when I have nothing to talk about."

❊ ❊ ❊

To Miss Grace Bedell
October 19, 1860:

My dear little Miss:
Your very agreeable letter of the 15th is received.
I regret the necessity of saying I have no daughters. I have three sons—one seventeen, one nine, and one seven years of age. They, with their mother, constitute my whole family.
As to the whiskers, having never worn any, do you not think people would call it a piece of silly affection if I were to begin it now? Your very sincere well-wisher.

❊ ❊ ❊

When he presented Coles County relatives with a sad-faced photograph of himself, he said, "This is not a very good-looking picture, but it's the best that could be produced from the poor subject."

❊ ❊ ❊

October 12th, 1863

Mrs. Alice C. Smith
Boston, Mass.
I shall have to acknowledge very briefly your letter informing me of the prosperity of your little boy whom you so kindly

named after me. You may rest assured that my little namesake has my best wishes that he may grow to be a good man and a good citizen. Yours Very Truly

✿   ✿   ✿

A procession had met Lincoln in Knoxville. One man in the crowd held up a lantern to show Lincoln's face, and Lincoln opened his speech: "My friends, the less you see of me the better you will like me."

✿   ✿   ✿

Saying goodbye to Col. James Grant Wilson, who was leaving for New Orleans, Lincoln gave him an autographed recent Brady photograph of himself, saying, "Now, my dear Colonel, perhaps you will value this after I am gone."

✿   ✿   ✿

"If to be the head of Hell is as hard as what I have to undergo here, I could find it in my heart to pity Satan himself."

✿   ✿   ✿

Bob Allen, a Democratic candidate, came through New Salem and sort of allowed he could tell a few things about Abe Lincoln and Ninian W. Edwards, only it wouldn't be fair to tell them.

Lincoln wrote him: "I am told that during my absence last week you stated publicly that you were in possession of a fact or facts, which if known to the public would entirely destroy the prospects of N.W. Edwards and myself at the ensuing election, but that through favor to us you would forbear to divulge them. No one has needed favors more than I, and generally few have been less unwilling to accept them, but in this case favor to me would be injustice to the public, and therefore I must beg your pardon for declining it. That I once had the confidence of the people of Sangamon County is sufficiently evident; and if I have done anything, either by design or misadventure, which if

58

known would subject me to a forfeiture of that confidence, he that knows of that thing and conceals it, is a traitor to his country's interest. I find myself wholly unable to form any conjecture of what fact or facts, real or supposed, you spoke; but my opinion of your veracity will not permit me for a moment to doubt that you at least believed what you said. I am flattered with the personal regard you manifested for me; but I hope that on mature reflection you will view the public interest as a paramount consideration and therefore let the worse come. I assure you that the candid statement of fact on your part, however low it may sink me, shall never break the ties of personal friendship between us. I wish to answer to this, and you are at liberty to publish both if you choose."

No reply came from Allen; Lincoln's mention of "personal friendship" between himself and Allen was sarcasm; his friends alluded to Allen as "a bag of wind."

✿   ✿   ✿

After winning re-election and carrying every state except Kentucky, Delaware, and New Jersey, to a serenade on the White House lawn he read from a window a prepared response. "Not very graceful," he told John Hay, "but I am growing old enough not to care much for the manner of doing things."

HISTORY

From an 1838 speech to the Young Men's Lyceum:

"Theirs was the task
(and nobly they performed it)
   to possess themselves,
      and through themselves, us,
         of this goodly land;
   and to uprear upon its hills
      and its valleys
         a political edifice of liberty
         and of equal rights;
"'tis ours only
to transmit these,
   the former, unprofaned by the foot of an invader,
   the latter, undecayed by the lapse of time,
      untorn by usurpation—
         to the latest generation that fate shall
            permit
         the world to know."

❂   ❂   ❂

To William Herndon:

Kings had always been involving and impoverishing their people in wars, pretending generally, if not always, that the good of the people was the object. This our convention understood to be the most oppressive of all kingly oppressions, and they resolved to so frame the Constitution that no one man should hold the power of bringing this oppression upon us. But your view destroys the whole matter, and places our President where kings have always stood.

❂   ❂   ❂

Address at Cooper Institute, New York:

"John Brown's effort was peculiar. It was not a slave insurrection. It was an attempt by white men to get up a revolt among slaves, in which the slaves refused to participate. In fact, it was so absurd that the slaves, with all their ignorance, saw plainly enough it could not succeed. That affair, in its philosophy, corresponds with the many attempts, related in history, at the assassination of kings and emperors. An enthusiast broods over the oppression of a people till he fancies himself commissioned by Heaven to liberate them. He ventures the attempt, which ends in little else than his own execution."

✿ ✿ ✿

Regarding those who accomplished the American Revolution:

"But those histories are gone. They can be read no more forever. They were a fortress of strength; but what invading foeman could never do, the silent artillery of time has done—the leveling of its walls. They are gone. They were a forest of giant oaks; but the all-restless hurricane has swept over them, and left only here and there a lonely trunk, despoiled of its verdure, shorn of its foliage, unshading and unshaded, to murmur in a few more gentle breezes, and to combat with its mutilated limbs a few more ruder storms, then to sink and be no more."

✿ ✿ ✿

Regarding his "House Divided" speech:

"If I had to draw a pen across my record and erase my whole life from sight, and I had one poor gift or choice left as to what I should save from the wreck, I should choose that speech and leave it to the world unerased."

✿ ✿ ✿

61

Speaking at Independence Hall:

"I am filled with deep emotion at finding myself standing in this place, where were collected together the wisdom, the patriotism, the devotion to principle, from which sprang the institutions under which we live."

       ✿   ✿   ✿

Annual Message to Congress
December 1, 1862:

"Fellow-citizens, *we* cannot escape history. We of this Congress and this administration, will be remembered in spite of ourselves. No personal significance, or insignificance, can spare one or another of us. The fiery trial through which we pass, will light us down, in honor or dishonor, to the latest generation. We *say* we are for the Union. The world will not forget that we say this. We know how to save the Union. The world knows we do know how to save it. We—even we *here*—hold the power, and bear the responsibility. In *giving* freedom to the *slave*, we *assure* freedom to the *free*—honorable alike in what we give, and what we preserve. We shall nobly save, or meanly lose, the last best hope of earth. Other means may succeed; this could not fail. The way is lain, peaceful, generous, just—a way which, if followed, the world will forever applaud, and God must forever bless."

HUMOR

"I laugh because if I didn't I would weep."

       ❀   ❀   ❀

To Brooks he quoted the English wit Sydney Smith in reference to one cabinet member: "It required a surgical operation to get a joke into his head."

       ❀   ❀   ❀

Regarding the satirical "Petroleum B. Nasby":

"For the genius to write these things, I would gladly give up my office."

"I am going to write Petroleum to come down here and I intend to tell him if he will communicate his talent to me, I will swap places with him."

       ❀   ❀   ❀

There are several versions of this one:

Senator Sumner strolled in to find Lincoln polishing his own boots.

SUMNER: Why, Mr. President, do you black your own boots?
LINCOLN: Whose boots did you think I blacked?

       ❀   ❀   ❀

Talk came from New York about a scheme to take the city out of the union and set up a free city. "I reckon," Lincoln remarked to a New Yorker, "it will be some time before the Front Door sets up housekeeping on its own account."

       ❀   ❀   ❀

In a letter to Levi Davis, Esq. of Vandalia, Lincoln wrote:

We have generally in this Country, Peace, Health and Plenty of no News.

LABOR

October 17, 1861:

Majr. Ramsay

My dear Sir
   The lady—bearer of this—says she has two sons who want to work. Set them at it, if possible. Wanting to work is so rare a merit, that it should be encouraged. Yours truly,

✿   ✿   ✿

He had heard Southern men declare that slaves were better off in the South than hired laborers in the North.

   "There is no permanent class of hired laborers amongst us. Twenty-five years ago I was a hired laborer. The hired laborer of today labors on his own account today, and will hire others to labor for him tomorrow.
   "Although volume upon volume is written to prove slavery a good thing, we never heard of the man who wishes to take the good of it by being a slave himself.
   "As labor is the common burden of our race, so the effort of some to shift the burden onto the shoulders of others is the great durable curse of the race."

✿   ✿   ✿

New Haven, 1860, referring to a local strike:

   "Now be it understood that I do not pretend to know all about the matter. I am merely going to speculate a little about some of its phases. And at the outset, *I am glad to see that a system of labor prevails in New England under which laborers CAN strike* when they want to, where they are not obliged to work under all circumstances, and are not tied down and

64

obliged to labor whether you pay them or not! I *like* the system which lets a man quit when he wants to, and wish it might prevail everywhere. One of the reasons why I am opposed to slavery is just here. What is the true condition of the laborer? I take it that it is best for all to leave each man free to acquire property as fast as he can. Some will get wealthy. I don't believe in a law to prevent a man from getting rich; it would do more harm than good. So while we do not propose any war upon capital, we do wish to allow the humblest man an equal chance to get rich with everybody else. When one starts poor, as most do in the race of life, free society is such that he knows he can better his condition; he knows that there is no fixed condition of labor, for his whole life. I am not shamed to confess that 25 years ago I was a hired laborer, mauling rails, at work on a flat-boat—just what might happen to any poor man's son! I want every man to have the chance—and I believe a black man is entitled to it—in which he *can* better his condition—when he may look forward and hope to be a hired laborer this year and the next, work for himself afterward, and finally to hire men to work for him. That is the true system."

LAW

From a letter to U.F. Linder
February 20, 1848:

In law it is good policy never to plead what you need not, but you oblige yourself to prove what you cannot.

✿ ✿ ✿

From a speech to the Young Men's Lyceum of Springfield
January 27, 1838:

"Let reverence for the laws be breathed by every American mother, to the lisping babe that prattles on her lap; let it be taught in schools, in seminaries, and in colleges; let it be written in primers, spelling books, and in almanacs; let it be preached from the pulpit, proclaimed in legislative halls, and enforced in halls of justice. And, in short, let it become the political religion of the nation."

✿ ✿ ✿

Annual message to Congress, December 3, 1861:

"It seems to be very important that the statute laws should be made as plain and intelligible as possible, and be reduced to as small a compass as may consist with the fullness and precision of the will of the legislature and the perspicuity of its language. This, well done, would, I think, greatly facilitate the labors of those whose duty it is to assist in the administration of the laws, and would be a lasting benefit to the people, by placing before them, in a more accessible and intelligible form, the laws which so deeply concern their interest and their duties."

✿ ✿ ✿

From a letter to Erastus Corning and Others
June 12, 1863:

A jury too frequently has at least one member more ready to hang the panel than to hang the traitor.

LAWYERS

Commenting on another lawyer, Lincoln once quipped: "He can compress the most words into the smallest ideas better than any man I ever met."

☼   ☼   ☼

Commenting on a fellow lawyer who always talked in a very loud voice, Lincoln remarked:

"Back in the days when I performed my part as a keelboat-man, I made the acquaintance of a trifling little steamboat which used to bustle and puff and wheeze about the Sangamon River. It had a five-foot boiler and seven-foot whistle, and every time it whistled, it stopped."

☼   ☼   ☼

To a young lawyer as the jury was filing out to vote on the case of a slippery client: "Better try and get your money now; if the jury comes in with a verdict for him, you won't get anything."

☼   ☼   ☼

In a letter recommending a young man applying for admission to the bar, Lincoln wrote the following note to a Judge Logan, a member of the bar's examining committee:

My dear Judge:
The bearer of this is a young man who thinks he can be a lawyer. Examine him if you want to. I have done so and am satisfied. He's a good deal smarter than he looks to be.
Yours,
Lincoln

☼   ☼   ☼

To counter a charge that he had made some errors in judgment, Lincoln once told a story about a lawyer and a minister who were arguing.

As they rode down the road together, the minister said, "Sir, do you ever make mistakes while in court?"

"Very rarely," the lawyer sniffed, "but on occasion, I must admit that I do."

"And what do you do when you make a mistake?" asked the minister.

"Why, if they are large mistakes, I mend them. If they are small, I let them go. Tell me, don't you ever make mistakes while preaching?"

"Of course," said the preacher. "And I dispose of them in the same way that you do. Not long ago, I meant to tell the congregation that the devil was the father of liars, but I made a mistake and said the father of lawyers. The mistake was so small that I let it go."

ABRAHAM LINCOLN, ATTORNEY AT LAW

I am not an accomplished lawyer. I find quite as much material for a lecture, in those points wherein I have failed, as in those wherein I have been moderately successful.

The leading rule for the lawyer, as for the man of every other calling, is diligence. Leave nothing for tomorrow which can be done today. Never let your correspondence fall behind. Whatever piece of business you have in hand, before stopping, do all the labor pertaining to it which can then be done. When you bring a common law suit, if you have the facts for doing so, write the declaration at once. If a law point be involved, examine the books, and note the authority you rely on upon the declaration itself, where you are sure to find it when wanted. The same of defense and pleas. In business not likely to be litigated—ordinary collection case, foreclosures, partitions, and the like—make all examinations of titles, and note them, and even draft orders and decrees in advance. This course has a triple advantage; it avoids omissions and neglect, saves your labor when once done, performs the labor out of court when you have leisure, rather than in court when you have not. Extemporaneous speaking should be practiced and cultivated. It is the lawyer's avenue to the public. However able and faithful he may be in other respects, people are slow to bring him business if he cannot make a speech. And yet there is not a more fatal error to young lawyers than relying too much on speech-making. If anyone, upon his rare powers of speaking, shall claim an exemption from the drudgery of the law, his case is a failure in advance.

Discourage litigation. Persuade your neighbors to compromise whenever you can. Point out to them how the *nominal* winner is often a *real* loser—in fees, and expenses, and waste of time. As a peace-maker the lawyer has a superior opportunity of being a good man. There will still be business enough.

Never stir up litigation. A worse man can scarcely be found than one who does this. Who can be more nearly a fiend than he who habitually overhauls the Register of Deeds, in search of defects in titles, whereon to stir up strife, and put money in his pocket? A moral tone ought to be infused into the profession, which should drive such men out of it.

The matter of fees is important far beyond the mere question of bread and butter involved. Properly attended to, fuller justice is done to both lawyer and client. An exorbitant fee should never be claimed. As a general rule, never take your whole fee in advance, nor any more than a small retainer. When fully paid beforehand, you are more than a common mortal if you can feel the same interest in the case, as if something was still in prospect for you, as well as for your client. And when you lack interest in the case, the job will very likely lack skill and diligence in the performance. Settle the *amount* of fee, and take a note in advance. Then you will feel that you are working for something, and you are sure to do your work faithfully and well. Never sell a fee note—at least not before the consideration service is performed. It leads to negligence and dishonesty—negligence by losing interest in the case, and dishonesty in refusing to refund when you have allowed the consideration to fail.

There is a vague popular belief that lawyers are necessarily dishonest. I say *vague*, because when we consider to what extent *confidence*, and *honors* are reposed in, and conferred upon lawyers by the people, it appears improbable that their *impression* of dishonesty is very distinct and vivid. Yet the impression is common—almost universal. Let no young man, choosing the law for a calling, for a moment yield to this popular belief. Resolve to be honest at all events; and if, in your own judgment, you can not be an honest lawyer, resolve to be honest without being a lawyer. Choose some other occupation, rather than one in the choosing of which you do, in advance, consent to be a knave.

From *Notes on the Practice of Law*
(circa 1850)

❧   ❧   ❧

Lincoln visited the courts in Cincinnati and enjoyed watching Bellamy Storer, a judge of the Superior Court, who had careless manners and direct methods. Lincoln took it all in, and remarked: "I wish we had that judge in Illinois. I think he would share with me the fatherhood of the legal jokes of the Illinois bar."

✿ ✿ ✿

When a rapscallion claimed money was owing him and hired Lincoln to prove it, the opposition lawyer brought in a receipt showing the money had been paid. Lincoln left the courtroom and was sitting in the hotel office with his feet on the stove when word came that he was wanted at court. "Tell the judge," he said, "that I can't come; I have to wash my hands."

✿ ✿ ✿

A fuddy-duddy judge corrected Lincoln's pronunciation of the word "lien" as "lean," saying it should be as "lion." In a minute or two Lincoln again pronounced the word his way, and, again being corrected, apologized. After slipping again, and the judge again correcting, Lincoln replied, "If my client had known there was a *lion* on his farm he wouldn't have stayed there long enough to bring this suit."

✿ ✿ ✿

Jas. S. Irwin Esqr.
Springfield, November 2, 1842

Owing to my absence, yours of the 22nd. ult. was not received till this moment.

Judge Logan & myself are willing to attend to any business in the Supreme Court you may send us. As to fees, it is impossible to establish a rule that will apply in all, or even a great many cases. We believe we are never accused of being very unreasonable in this particular; and we would always be easily satisfied, provided we could see the money—but whatever fees we earn at a distance, if not paid *before*, we have noticed we never hear of after the work is done. We therefore, are growing a little sensitive on that point.

❈　❈　❈

In one case Lincoln argued that the railroad corporation he was defending in a damage suit had more of a soul than a lying witness who brought the damage suit. The opposing lawyer had said his client had a soul and the railroad hadn't. Lincoln replied: "But our client is but a conventional name for thousands of widows and orphans whose husbands' and parents' hard earnings are represented by this defendant, and who possess souls which they would not swear away as the plaintiff has done for ten million times as much as is at stake here."

Lincoln tried to remind the jury of the farmers who in that time had mortgaged their farms and the farmers' wives who often had subscribed their butter-and-egg money to get a railroad connecting them with better markets.

❈　❈　❈

When his annual pass on the Alton Railroad was used up, he wrote the superintendent: "Says John to Tom, 'Here's your old rotten wheelbarrow. I've broke it usin' on it. I wish you would mend it, 'case I shall want to borrow it this afternoon.' Acting on this as a precedent, I say, 'Here's your old "chalked hat." I wish you would take it and send me a new one, 'case I shall want to use it by the 1st of March.' "

❈　❈　❈

Lincoln had a habit of stashing documents away in odd places. After his death, law partner Herndon found a bundle of papers marked:

"When you can't find it anywhere else, look here."

❈　❈　❈

72

After hearing many theories and noisy wrangling in a big law case, Lincoln walked out on the Rock Island Bridge, and came upon a boy with a fishing-pole. "I suppose you know all about this river," he ventured. The boy answered, "I guess I do. It was here when I was born, and it's been here ever since." And Lincoln smiled, "I'm mighty glad I walked out here where there is not so much opinion and a little more fact."

✿ ✿ ✿

Fine legal points and boring details did not interest Lincoln. "If I can free this case from technicalities and get it properly swung to the jury, I'll win it," he often said.

✿ ✿ ✿

The widow of a Revolutionary War soldier told Lincoln that a pension agent named Wright had got her a payment from the Federal Government amounting to $400—and kept half of it for himself as a commission. Lincoln told Herndon, "I am going to skin Wright and get that money back." He brought suit and put the tottering widow on the witness stand, where she told her story through tears.

He told the jury, "She was not always thus. She was once a beautiful young woman. Her step was as elastic, her face as fair, and her voice as sweet as any that rang in the mountains of old Virginia. But now she is poor and defenseless. Out here on the prairies of Illinois, many hundreds of miles from the scenes of her childhood, she appeals to us, who enjoy the privileges achieved for us by the patriots of the Revolution, and for our sympathetic aid and manly protection. All I ask is, shall we befriend her?" He pictured the sufferings of the soldiers of the Revolutionary War, and scored the defendant fiercely.

Some of the jurymen wept. The verdict gave the widow the full amount of money Wright had taken from her. Lincoln paid her hotel bill, bought her a railroad ticket back home, and later sent her the full amount of pension money—with no charge for lawyers' fees.

Herndon had picked up Lincoln's notes. They read: "No contract.—No professional services.—Unreasonable charge.—Money retained by Def't not given by Pl'ff.—Revolutionary War.—Describe Valley Forge Privations.—Ice.—Soldier's bleeding feet.—Pl'ff's husband.—Soldier leaving home for army.—Skin def't.—Close."

✿　✿　✿

A widow came into the office of Stuart & Lincoln for help. She had come to Springfield to sell ten acres of land left by her husband, but she found that General James Adams claimed the land had been signed over to him by the husband for a debt owed Adams as a lawyer. Lincoln worked on the case, searched the records, then published a handbill opening with: "It is well known to most of you, that there is existing at this time, considerable excitement in regard to General Adams's titles to certain tracts of land, and the manner in which he acquired them."

He went into the fact that Adams had falsified documents in order to swindle "a widow woman" out of ten acres of land. Adams wrote a reply which filled six newspaper columns, and Lincoln replied with a one-column answer analyzing affidavits offered by Adams, saying they were "all false as hell," and adding: "In conclusion I will only say that I have a character to defend as well as Gen. Adams, but I disdain to whine about it as he does."

Adams again filled six newspaper columns with his defense. Lincoln commented: "Let it be remembered that when he first came to this country he attempted to impose himself upon the community as a lawyer, and actually carried the attempt so far as to induce a man who was under a charge of murder to entrust the defense of his life in his hands, and finally took his money and got him hanged. Is this the man that is to raise a breeze in his favor by abusing lawyers? If he is not himself a lawyer, it is for the lack of sense, and not of inclination. If he is not a lawyer, he *is* a liar, for he proclaimed himself a lawyer, and got a man hanged by depending on him."

LIBERTY

Address at Sanitary Fair, Baltimore
April 18, 1864:

"The world has never had a good definition of the word liberty, and the American people, just now, are much in want of one. We all declare for liberty; but in using the same *word* we do not all mean the same *thing*. With some the word liberty may mean for each man to do as he pleases with himself, and the product of his labor; while with others the same word may mean for some men to do as they please with other men, and the product of other men's labor. Here are two, not only different, but incompatible things, called by the same name—liberty. And it follows that each of the things is, by the respective parties, called by two different and incompatible names—liberty and tyranny.

"The shepherd drives the wolf from the sheep's throat, for which the sheep thanks the shepherd as a liberator, while the wolf denounces him for the same act as the destroyer of liberty, especially as the sheep was a black one. Plainly the sheep and the wolf are not agreed upon a definition of the word liberty; and precisely the same difference prevails today among us human creatures, even in the North, and all professing to love liberty."

✵   ✵   ✵

To Joshua F. Speed
August 24, 1855:

Our progress in degeneracy appears to me to be pretty rapid. As a nation, we began by declaring that *"all men are created equal."* We now practically read it "all men are created equal, *except Negroes.*" When the Know-Nothings get control, it will read "all men are created equal, except Negroes, *and*

75

foreigners, and catholics." When it comes to this I should prefer emigrating to some country where they make no pretence of loving liberty—to Russia, for instance, where despotism can be taken pure, and without the base alloy of hypocracy.

LOVE

"My wife is as handsome as when she was a girl, and I, a poor nobody then, fell in love with her; and what is more I have never fallen out."

○ ○ ○

Letter to Joshua Speed:

I know what the painful point with you is at all times when you are unhappy; it is an apprehension that you do not love her as you should. What nonsense! How came you to court her? Was it because you thought she deserved it, and that you had given her reason to expect it? If it was for that, why did not the same reason make you court at least twenty others of whom you can think, and to whom it would apply with greater force than to her? Did you court her for her wealth? Why, you know she had none. But you say you reasoned yourself into it. What do you mean by that? Was it not that you found yourself unable to reason yourself out of it? Did you not think and partly form the purpose of courting her the first time you ever saw her or heard of her? There was nothing at that time for reason to work upon. Whether she was moral, amiable, sensible, or even of good character, you did not, nor could then know, except, perhaps you might infer the last from the company you found her in. All you then did or could know of her was her personal appearance and deportment; and these, if they impress at all, impress the heart, and not the head.

Say candidly, were not those heavenly black eyes the whole basis of all your early reasoning on the subject? Did you not go and take me all the way to Lexington and back, for no other purpose but to get to see her again? What earthly consideration would you take to find her scouting and despising you, and giving herself up to another? But of this you have no apprehension; and therefore you cannot bring it home to your feelings. I shall be so anxious about you that I shall want you to write by every mail.

○ ○ ○

Another letter to Joshua Speed, February 25, 1842
(after Speed's marriage):

My old father used to have a saying, "If you make a bad bargain, hug it all the tighter," and it occurs to me that if the bargain you have just closed can possibly be called a bad one, it is certainly the most pleasant one for applying that maxim to which my fancy can by any effort picture.

❀   ❀   ❀

Another letter to Speed:

I always was superstitious; I believe God made me one of the instruments of bringing your Fanny and you together, which union I have no doubt he had foreordained. Whatever he designs he will do for me yet.

THE MEDIA

"In times like the present, men should utter nothing for which they would not willingly be responsible through time and in eternity."

✿   ✿   ✿

On the night after his re-election in November, Lincoln had come into the White House parlor with a little roll of manuscript in his hand, saying to Noah Brooks: "I know what you are thinking about. But there's no claptrap about me. And I am free to say that in the excitement of the moment I am sure to say something which I am sorry for when I see it in print. So I have it here in black and white, and there are no mistakes made. People attach too much importance to what I say anyhow."

✿   ✿   ✿

Frederick Maryland
October 4, 1862:

"In my present position it is hardly proper for me to make speeches. Every word is so closely noted that it will not do to make trivial ones, and I cannot be expected to be prepared to make a matured one just now. If I were as I have been most of my life, I might perhaps talk amusing to you for half an hour, and it wouldn't hurt anybody; but as it is, I can only return my sincere thanks for the compliment paid our cause and our common country."

✿   ✿   ✿

A dispatch from General Schenck reported a skirmish in Virginia, with thirty prisoners taken, all armed with Colt's revolvers. Lincoln read it and with a twinkle in his eye said that with customary newspaper exaggeration of army news they might be sure in the next day's prints that "all the little Colt's revolvers would have grown into horse-pistols."

❋ ❋ ❋

"Everything I say, you know, goes into print. If I make a mistake it doesn't merely affect me or you, but the country. I therefore ought at least try not to make mistakes."

(1864)

MONEY

"Wealth is simply a superfluity of things we don't need."

❖   ❖   ❖

After the Lincoln-Douglas debates, Lincoln wrote a friend in November 1858:

I am the poorest hand living to get others to pay. I have been on expenses so long without earning any thing that I am absolutely without money now for even household purposes.

❖   ❖   ❖

From a letter to Joshua Speed:

I am so poor and make so little headway in the world, that I drop back in a month of idleness as much as I gain in a year's sowing.

❖   ❖   ❖

A lease on a valuable hotel property in Quincy was handled by Lincoln for George P. Floyd, who mailed a check for twenty-five dollars, to which Lincoln replied:

Mr. George P. Floyd,
Quincy, Illinois
February 21, 1856

Dear Sir:
I have just received yours of 16th, with check on Flagg & Savage for twenty-five dollars. You must think I am a high-priced man. You are too liberal with your money.
Fifteen dollars is enough for the job. I send you a receipt for fifteen dollars, and return to you a ten dollar bill. Yours truly.

❖   ❖   ❖

In the town of Danville, Lincoln's law partner there, Ward Hill Lamon, brought the case of a girl named Scott, who was, as was said, "not in her right mind." She had $10,000 in property, mostly cash, and a schemer had struck up an acquaintance with her and asked her to marry him. Her brother wanted a conservator appointed by the court to take care of her and her property, and had agreed with Lamon to pay a fee of $250 when the case was won. On trial it took Lincoln and Lamon only twenty minutes to win their case, and Lamon was paid $250. Lincoln was sore and hurt, and forced Lamon to give back to Miss Scott half of the $250.

Judge Davis said, "Lincoln, you are impoverishing this bar by your picayune charges of fees, and the lawyers have reason to complain of you." Lincoln stuck to the point: "That money comes out of the pocket of a poor, demented girl, and I would rather starve than swindle her in this manner."

❈   ❈   ❈

In cooperation with a Chicago lawyer, Lincoln saved a farm in Brown County for Isaac Hawley, a Springfield man, and Hawley had fifty dollars ready to pay the fee. Lincoln smiled at Hawley and said, "Well, Isaac, I think I will charge you about ten dollars." To another client, he said, "I will charge you twenty-five dollars, and if you think that is too much I will make it less."

NEGROES

"I believed the indispensable necessity for military emancipation and arming the blacks would come, unless averted."

❀   ❀   ❀

"All I ask for the Negro is that, if you do not like him, let him alone. If God gave him but little, that little let him enjoy.

"Certainly the negro is not our equal in color—perhaps not in many other respects; still, in the right to put into his mouth the bread that his own hands have earned, he is the equal of every other man, white or black. In pointing out that more has been given you, you cannot be justified in taking away the little which has been given him."

❀   ❀   ❀

He appealed to the voters to "discard all this quibbling about this man and the other man—this race and that race and the other race as being inferior. There is no reason in the world why the Negro is not entitled to all the natural rights enumerated in the Declaration of Independence, the right to life, liberty, and the pursuit of happiness. I hold that he is as much entitled to these as the white man."

❀   ❀   ❀

Polly, a free Negro woman working in Springfield, came to the Lincoln & Herndon law office one day. Her boy had been hired as a steamboat hand down the Mississippi, and, arriving in New Orleans without his freedom papers, had been put in jail. Lincoln and Herndon went to the governor of Illinois, who said he could do nothing, and then wrote to the governor of Louisiana, who said he could take no action. The two lawyers headed a subscription list and raised the cash that bought the Negro boy's freedom. And Herndon said Lincoln had told the governor of Illinois, "By God, governor, I'll make the ground in this country too hot for the foot of a slave, whether you release this boy or not."

* * *

June 26, 1857 (in a speech regarding Dred Scott):

"How differently the respective courses of the Democratic and Republican parties incidentally bear on the question of forming a will—a public sentiment—for colonization, is easy to see. The Republicans inculcate, with whatever of ability they can, that the Negro is a man; that his bondage is cruelly wrong, and that the field of his oppression ought not be enlarged. The Democrats deny his manhood; deny, or dwarf to insignificance, the wrong of his bondage; so far as possible, crush all sympathy for him; compliment themselves as Union-savers for doing so; and call the indefinite outspreading of his bondage 'a sacred right of self-government.'

"The plainest print cannot be read through a gold eagle; and it will be ever hard to find many men who will send a slave to Liberia, and pay his passage, while they can send him to a new country, Kansas for instance, and sell him for fifteen hundred dollars, and the rise."

* * *

Speech at Charleston, Illinois, during the Lincoln-Douglas campaign:

"I will say then that I am not nor ever had been in favor of bringing about in any way the social and political equality of the white and black races—that I am not nor ever have been in favor of making voters or jurors of Negroes nor of qualifying them to hold office, nor of intermarrying with white people; and I will say, in addition to this, that there is a physical difference between the white and black races which I believe will forever forbid the two races living together on terms of political and social equality. And inasmuch as they cannot so live, while they do remain together there must be the position of superior and inferior, and I as much as any other man am in favor of having the superior position assigned to the white race. I say upon this occasion I do not perceive that because the white man is to have the superior position the Negro should be denied everything. I do not understand that because I do not want a Negro woman for a slave I must necessarily want her for a wife."

❖ ❖ ❖

And he came to the matter of Judge Douglas being horrified at the mixing of blood by the white and black races. He too would be horrified. "Agreed for once—a thousand times agreed. There are white men enough to marry all the white women, and black men enough to marry all the black women; and so let them be married."

But he wished to note there were 405,751 mulattoes in the United States in 1850. "Nearly all have sprung from black slaves and white masters."

He quoted statistics, and argued that the Supreme Court by its decision in degrading black people was promoting race amalgamation. "Could we have had our way, the chances of these black girls ever mixing their blood with that of white people would have been diminished at least to the extent that it could not have been without their consent. But Judge Douglas is delighted to have them decided to be slaves, and not human enough to have a hearing, even if they were free, and thus left subject to the forced concubinage of their masters, and liable to become the mothers of mulattoes in spite of themselves; the very state of case that produces nine-tenths of all the mulattoes—all the mixing of blood in the nation."

"Judge Douglas will have it that I want a Negro wife. He never can be brought to understand that there is any middle ground on this subject. I have lived until my fiftieth year, and have never had a Negro woman either for a slave or a wife, and I think I can live fifty centuries, for that matter, without having had one or either."

❖ ❖ ❖

From letter to Hon. James C. Conkling
August 26, 1863:

You say you will not fight to free Negroes. Some of them seem willing to fight for you; but, no matter. Fight you, then, exclusively to save the Union. I issued the proclamation on purpose to aid you in saving the Union. Whenever you shall have conquered all resistance to the Union, if I shall urge you to continue fighting, it will be an apt time, then, for you to declare you will not fight to free Negroes.

❖ ❖ ❖

Thousands of black soldiers were now fighting and dying in the Union ranks.

"You say you will not fight to free Negroes. Some of them seem willing to fight for you. . . . Why should they do anything for us, if we will do nothing for them? If they stake their lives for us, they must be prompted by the strongest motive—even the promise of freedom. And the promise being made, must be kept."

❖ ❖ ❖

To Andrew Johnson
March 26, 1863:

My dear sir:
I am told you have at least *thought* of raising a Negro military force. In my opinion the country now needs no specific thing so much as some man of your ability, and position, to go to this work. When I speak of your position, I mean that of an eminent

86

citizen of a slave-state, and himself a slave-holder. The colored population is the great available and yet unavailed of, force for restoring the Union. The bare sight of fifty thousand armed, and drilled black soldiers on the banks of the Mississippi, would end the rebellion at once. And who doubts that we can present that sight, if we but take hold in earnest? If you have been thinking of it please do not dismiss the thought. Yours truly

✿   ✿   ✿

Recognizing a superiority of black freedom fighters to white shirkers:

"And then [when peace comes], there will be some black men who can remember that, with silent tongue, and clenched teeth, and steady eye, and well-poised bayonet, they have helped mankind on to this consummation; while, I fear, there will be some white ones, unable to forget that, with indignant heart and deceitful speech, they have strove to hinder it."

✿   ✿   ✿

Once as the presidential party drove around the encampments, they came upon a little settlement of tents and shanties. It was a camp of colored refugees who flocked out eagerly to yell, "Hurrah for Massa Linkum." Mrs. Lincoln, with a warm friendly glance at the numerous children, asked her husband how many of them he supposed were named Abraham Lincoln. The President answered, "Let's see; this is April 1863. I should say that of all those babies under two years of age, perhaps two-thirds have been named for me."

✿   ✿   ✿

To Charles Sumner
May 19, 1864:

My dear Sir:

The bearer of this is the widow of Major Booth, who fell at Fort Pillow. She makes a point, which I think very worthy of consideration which is, widows and children *in fact*, of colored soldiers who fall in our service, be placed in law, the same as if their marriages were legal, so that they can have the benefit of the provisions made the widows & orphans of white soldiers. Please see & hear Mrs. Booth. Yours truly.

*   *   *

To John Glenn
February 7, 1865:

Lt. Col. Glenn
Commanding Post at Henderson, Ky.

*   *   *

Complaint is made to me that you are forcing Negroes into the Military service, and even torturing them—riding them on rails and the like—to extort their consent. I hope this may be a mistake. The like must not be done by you, or any one under you. You must not force Negroes any more than white men. Answer me on this.

*   *   *

Speech to the 140th Indiana Regiment, Washington, D.C.:

"Fellow citizens—it will be but a very few words that I shall undertake to say. I was born in Kentucky, raised in Indiana and lived in Illinois. And now I am here, where it is my business to care equally for the good people of all the States. I am glad to see an Indiana regiment on this day able to present the captured flag to the Governor of Indiana. I am not disposed, in saying this, to make a distinction between the States, for all have done equally well. There are but few views or aspects of this great war upon which I have not said or written something whereby my own opinions might be known. But there is one— the recent attempt by our erring brethren, as they are sometimes called—to employ the Negro to fight for them. I have neither written nor made a speech on that subject, because that was their business, not mine; and if I had a wish upon the subject I had not the power to introduce it, or make it effective. The great question with them was, whether the Negro, being put into the army, would fight for them. I do not know, and therefore cannot decide. They ought to know better than we. I have in my lifetime heard many arguments why the Negroes ought to be slaves; but if they fight for those who would keep them in slavery it will be a better argument than any I have yet heard. He who will fight for that ought to be a slave. They have concluded at last to take one out of four of the slaves, and put them in the army; and that one out of the four who will fight to keep the others in slavery ought to be a slave himself unless he is killed in a fight. While I have often said that all men ought to be free, yet I would allow those colored persons to be slaves who want to be; and next to them those white persons who argue in favor of making other people slaves. I am in favor of giving an opportunity to such white men to try it on for themselves. I will say one thing in regard to the Negro being employed to fight for them. I do know he cannot fight and stay at home and make bread too—and as one is about as important as the other to them, I don't care which they do. I am rather in favor of having them try as soldiers. They lack one vote of doing that, and I wish I could send my vote over the river so that I might cast it in favor of allowing the Negro to fight. But they cannot fight and work both. We must now see the bottom of the enemy's resources. They will stand out as long as they can, and if the Negro will fight for them, they must allow him to fight. They have drawn upon their last branch of resources. And we can now see the bottom. I am glad to see the end so near at hand. I have said now more than I intended, and will therefore bid you goodby."

(March 17, 1865)

NORTH AND SOUTH

"A house divided against itself cannot stand. . . . Our cause must be intrusted to, and conducted by its own undoubted friends—whose hands are free, whose hearts are in the work— who do care for the result."

(From House Divided speech, June 16, 1858)

❉ ❉ ❉

"The fact is the people have not yet made up their minds that we are at war with the South. They have not buckled down to the determination to fight this war through; for they have got the idea into their heads that we are going to get out of this fix somehow by strategy! That's the word—*strategy*! General McClellan thinks he is going to whip the Rebels by strategy; and the army has got the same notion. They have no idea that the war is to be carried on and put through by hard, tough fighting, that it will hurt somebody; and no headway is going to be made while this delusion lasts."

❉ ❉ ❉

The seizure early in the war of copies of dispatches in major telegraph offices uncovered names of individuals who had expressed disloyalties to an extent shocking, even appalling. Lincoln thought of an Illinois farmer who for years had prized and loved an elm tree that spread its majestic branches near his home. Chasing a squirrel one day, the farmer saw the animal scurry up the elm's trunk and disappear in a hole. Looking further, the farmer found the tree to be hollow, the whole inside rotten, the tree ready to fall at the next wind storm. Lincoln quoted the farmer as moaning to his wife, "My God! I wish I had never seen that squirrel!" And pointing to the piles of telltale copies of dispatches, he said, "And I wish we had never seen what we have seen today."

❉ ❉ ❉

Lincoln told Ward Lamon regarding the current turmoil between North and South:

"A man chased around a tree by a bull gained on the bull and got it by the tail. The bull pawed, snorted, broke into a run, the man after it still holding to the tail and bawling, 'Darn you, who commenced this fuss?'"

❖ ❖ ❖

To a New Yorker who remarked that the President of the United States and the President of the Confederacy were both born in the same state:

"Oh, I don't know about that. Those Kentucky people will tell you that they raise 'most anything in their State, and I reckon they're mighty near right."

❖ ❖ ❖

"It will do you good to get down to Washington," Joe Gillespie offered as cheer.

"I know it will," was Lincoln's answer. "I only wish I could have got there to lock the door before the horse was stolen. But when I get to the spot, I can find the tracks."

(1861)

❖ ❖ ❖

"In stating a single condition of peace, I mean simply to say, that the war will cease on the part of the government whenever it shall have ceased on the part of those who began it."

❖ ❖ ❖

Baltimore was heard from in delegates of the Young Men's Christian Association. The Rev. R. Fuller, spokesman, told Lincoln that his duty as a Christian statesman was to "recognize the independence of the Southern States." Lincoln looked them over and said:

91

"You, gentlemen, come here to me and ask for peace on any terms, and yet have no words of condemnation for those who are making war on us. You express great horror of bloodshed, and yet would not lay a straw in the way of those who are organizing in Virginia and elsewhere to capture this city. . . . You would have me break my oath and surrender the government without a blow. There is no Washington in that—no Jackson in that—there is no manhood or honor in that."

❋   ❋   ❋

Response to a serenade, Washington, D.C.
April 10, 1865:

". . . . I see you have a band of music with you. I propose closing up this interview by the band performing a particular tune which I will name. Before this is done, however, I wish to mention one or two little circumstances connected with it. I have always thought 'Dixie' one of the best tunes I have ever heard. Our adversaries over the way attempted to appropriate it, but I insisted yesterday that we fairly captured it. I presented the question to the Attorney General, and he gave it as his legal opinion that it is our lawful prize. I now request the band to favor me with its performance."

❋   ❋   ❋

Philosophy and the example of a strange, unhappy marriage were given the cabinet at one of its meetings when Lincoln had brought up the matter of shifting and trying new generals.

"This situation reminds me of a Union man in Kentucky whose two sons enlisted in the Federal Army. His wife was of Confederate sympathies. His nearest neighbor was a Confederate in feeling, and his two sons were fighting under Lee. This neighbor's wife was a Union woman and it nearly broke her heart to know that her sons were arrayed against the Union.

"Finally, the two men, after each had talked the matter over with his wife, agreed to obtain divorces; this they did, and the

Union man and the Union woman were wedded, as were the Confederate man and the Confederate woman—the men swapped wives, in short.

"But this didn't seem to help matters any, for the sons of the Union woman were still fighting for the South, and the sons of the Confederate woman continued in the Federal Army; the Union husband couldn't get along with his Union wife, and the Confederate husband and his Confederate wife couldn't agree upon anything, being forever fussing and quarreling."

OFFICE SEEKERS

"If our American society and the United States government are demoralized and overthrown, it will come from the voracious desire for office, this wriggle to live without toil, work, and labor, from which I am not free myself."

✿ ✿ ✿

To a man whom he later made paymaster:
"I'm making brigadier-generals today but I'll get around to your case later."

✿ ✿ ✿

A disgruntled office-seeker snorted, "Why, I am one of those who made you President!" And Lincoln replied, "Yes, and it's a pretty mess you got me into!"

✿ ✿ ✿

Regarding filling vacancies:

"There are twenty applicants, and of these I must make nineteen enemies."

✿ ✿ ✿

A dispute over a high-salaried Ohio postmastership brought several delegations to the White House, and papers piled high in behalf of two men about equally competent. One day—as the politicians told of the affair afterward—Lincoln was bored by still another delegation, more arguments, even more petitions. And he called to a clerk: "This matter has got to end somehow. Bring me a pair of scales." They were brought. "Now put in all the petitions and letters in favor of one man and see how much they weigh, and then weigh the other fellow's pile." It was done. One bundle weighed three-quarters of a pound more than the other.

"Make out an appointment," said the President, "for the man who has the heavier papers."

❃ ❃ ❃

A persistent party member once appeared before President Lincoln and demanded appointment to a judgeship as reward for some campaigning he'd done in Illinois. The President, aware of the man's lack of judicial attributes, told him it was impossible. "There are simply no vacancies at the present time," Mr. Lincoln said.

The man left. Early the next morning he was walking along the Potomac when he saw a drowned man pulled from the river and immediately recognized him as a federal judge. Without a moment of hesitation he presented himself to Mr. Lincoln while the President was eating breakfast, told him what he had seen, and demanded an immediate appointment to the vacancy.

Lincoln shook his head. "I'm sorry, sir, but you came too late," said the President. "I have already appointed the lawyer who saw him fall in."

❃ ❃ ❃

April 15, 1861

Mr. Huffman, Collector

If there is any secessionist in your department I wish you would remove him, and give the place to Mr. S. C. Atkinson; or, if, in any way you can give him a place, I shall be obliged.

❃ ❃ ❃

May 8, 1861

My dear sir:

I am told there is an office in your department called "The Superintending Architect of the Treasury Department, connected with the Bureau of Construction," which is now held by a man of the name of Young, and wanted by a gentleman of the name of Christopher Adams.

Ought Mr. Young to be removed, and if yea, ought Mr. Adams to be appointed? Mr. Adams is magnificently recommended; but the great point in his favor is that Thurlow Weed and Horace Greeley join in recommending him. I suppose the like never happened before, and never will again; so that it is now or never. What say you? Yours truly,

❆ ❆ ❆

July 4, 1861

Horatio N. Taft, the boy-bearer of this, wishes to be a page. By the within, his father seems to be willing; and, as he is a playmate of my little boys, I am quite willing.

❆ ❆ ❆

August 10, 1861
Hon. Sec. of War

My dear Sir
If Ohio is not already overstocked with paymasterships of Volunteers, let Richard P. L. Barber have one. I personally wish this done. Yours truly,

❆ ❆ ❆

Lincoln told a story of a certain king who called the court minister, said he wanted to go hunting, and asked the minister if it would rain. The minister told him the weather would be fair, it would not rain, and he could go hunting. On the way the royal party met a farmer riding a jackass. The farmer told the king to turn back, it was going to rain. The king laughed, went on, and no sooner got started hunting than a heavy downpour of rain drenched him and his party. The king went back to the palace, threw out the minister, and called for the farmer.

"Tell me how you knew it would rain."

"I did not know, Your Majesty, it's not me, it's my jackass. He puts his ears forward when it's going to be wet, and back when it's going to be dry weather."

The king sent the farmer away and had the jackass brought and put in the place of the Minister.

"It was here," said Lincoln, "the king made a great mistake."

"How so?"

"Why, ever since that time, every jackass wants an office!"

✿ ✿ ✿

One F. J. Whipple of New York, seated in the hall opposite the President's office, saw a man come from the private part of the White House. He arose and said, "This is Mr. Lincoln, I believe."

"Yes. What can I do for you?"

"Nothing, sir. You have not an office I would accept."

Lincoln slapped him on the shoulder. "Is it possible? Come into my office. I want to look at you. It is a curiosity to see a man who does not want an office. You might as well try to dip the Potomac dry as to satisfy them all."

They talked. The President idled with a pencil and paper. The notable visitor who wanted no office departed with a warm handshake. And a few days later the guard Crook heard a senator asking Lincoln what the pencil sketch on the desk was, and Lincoln said, "It is the portrait of the one man who does not want an office."

✿ ✿ ✿

A Canadian ornithologist, A.M. Ross, working confidentially with Lincoln and Sumner on foreign and Confederate movements against the North, called with important intercepted mail. It was midnight and he apologized to Lincoln for the hour. Lincoln was in good humor. "No, no! You did right. You may waken me whenever you please. I have slept with one eye open ever since I came to Washington; I never close both except when an office seeker is looking for me."

✿ ✿ ✿

An earnest Republican of proved deeds asked that his son be appointed an army paymaster. How old was the son?

"He is twenty—well, nearly twenty-one."

"Nearly twenty-one! I wouldn't appoint the angel Gabriel a paymaster if he wasn't twenty-one!"

❀ ❀ ❀

James B. Fry was in charge of the appointment branch of the Adjutant General's office. He noted that one day at the White House Lincoln confided: "I have here a bushel-basketful of applications for officers in the army. I have tried to examine them all, but they have increased so rapidly that I have got behind and may have neglected some. I'll send them to your office. Overhaul them, lay those that require further attention before the Secretary of War, and file the others."

Fry went through the basket, found the papers dotted with notes, comments, and queries by the President. He brought one back, as he supposed the President would not care to have it in the official files. Lincoln had written: "On this day Mrs. _____ called upon me. She is the wife of Major _____ of the regular army. She wants her husband made a brigadier-general. She is a saucy little woman, and I think she will torment me till I have to do it." Fry recalled this at a later time when the "little woman's" husband was named a brigadier.

❀ ❀ ❀

Carl Schurz noted the President as saying once in a heavy hour, "I have discovered a good way of providing officers for this government: put all the names of the applicants into one pepper-box and all the offices into another, then shake the two, and make appointments just as the names and offices happen to drop out together."

PARDONS

"It rests me, after a hard day's work, that I can find some excuse for saving some poor fellow's life."

❀   ❀   ❀

A father and mother came for help to get their two boys back home. They had tried all other ways and the President was their last hope. The two boys, both underage, had enlisted in the navy. The worst fault of the boys, said the parents, was their disobedience. Lincoln picked up a card and wrote to the Secretary of the Navy ordering their discharge on the grounds that "the United States don't need the services of boys who disobey their parents."

❀   ❀   ❀

Congressman Kellogg of New York brought to Lincoln's attention the affair of a helter-skelter lad who before the war served six months in the regular army, deserted, came home, told his father nothing about it, sobered up, and settled down. Later the boy volunteered at the beginning of the war, helped raise a regiment, was elected one of its officers, and in a charge across a bridge during one battle saw his colonel at his side killed and took wounds himself. Then an old-timer of the regular army recognized him, and let him know he would be exposed as a deserter. He managed to get furloughed home, told his father he would "die first" rather than be arrested as a deserter.

This in short was the story Kellogg told. Lincoln wasn't interested until the charge across the bridge.

"Do you say the young man was wounded?"

"Yes, badly."

"Then," mused Lincoln, "he has shed his blood for his country. Kellogg, isn't there something in scripture about the 'shedding of blood' being the 'remission of sins'?"

"Guess you're about right there."

"That's a good point, and there is no going behind it." The President took a pen and wrote a pardon without condition or reservation.

❁   ❁   ❁

In a crowded room near the President's office, a congressman noticed an old man crouched in a corner, sobbing. The next morning, he saw the old man there again, sobbing as the day before. He talked with him and then took him in to tell his story to the President. The man's son, who was with Butler's army, had been convicted of a crime and sentenced by court-martial to be shot. The President read the old man a telegram from General Butler protesting against executive interference with army court-martials. The old man was dazed a moment, then shook with a desperate grief. Lincoln watched a minute and said, "By jings, Butler or no Butler, here goes," and wrote a few words. He showed them to the old man; they were a Presidential order that the son was "not to be shot until further orders from me." The old man, still in grief, said, "I thought it was to be a pardon. But you say 'not to be shot till further orders,' and you may order him shot next week."

Lincoln smiled. "Well, my friend, I see you are not very well acquainted with me. If your son never lays eyes on death till further orders come from me to shoot him, he will live to be a great deal older than Methuselah."

❁   ❁   ❁

Noah Brooks wrote of how one day in the office of the Superintendent of Public Printing he saw a young woman enter with a card signed "A. Lincoln" telling Superintendent Defrees that "The bearer, a poor girl, has a brother in our lines, as a prisoner of war, who wishes to take an oath of allegiance. Be good enough to look into the facts and report to me." From the young woman came a story that her brother was forced into Confederate military service early in the war, that he had been unable to escape to the Union lines, that she believed his claim that he was a Union man from the first and should be released on his taking the oath of allegiance. "The girl had been turned away by the surly officials of the War Department," wrote Brooks, "but had got access to the President, whose kind heart was at once enlisted, and he determined that justice should be done, so he sent the sister to the kindly Defrees, who likes to do a generous act."

* * *

A rough rider of the Confederate Mosby's raiders awaited the firing squad while his wife came to Lincoln with her story. The President, knowing how fierce Mosby's men were in the field, asked her what kind of a husband her man was. Did he get drunk. Did he beat her and the children?

"No, no," said the wife. "He is a good man, a good husband. He loves me. He loves the children. And we can't live without him. The only trouble is that he is a fool about politics. I live in the North, born there, and if I can get him home he will do no more fighting for the South."

"Well," said Lincoln as he thumbed through the papers, "I will pardon your husband and turn him over to you for safe keeping."

Here the woman broke into tears, sobbing beyond control.

"My dear woman, if I had known how badly it was going to make you feel, I never would have pardoned him."

"You don't understand me," she cried in a fresh flow of tears.

"Yes, yes, I do. And if you don't go away at once I shall be crying with you."

* * *

To Edwin M. Stanton

July 28, 1863
Hon Secretary of War

A young son of the Senator Brown of Mississippi, not yet twenty, as I understand, was wounded, and made a prisoner at

Gettysburg. His mother is sister of Mrs. P. R. Fendall of this city. Mr. Fendall, on behalf of himself and family, asks that he and they may have charge of the boy, to cure him up, being responsible for his person and good behavior. Would it not be rather a grateful and graceful thing to let them have him? Yours truly

* * *

He pardoned a deserter, signing his name with the comment, "Well, I think this boy can do us more good above ground than under ground."

* * *

The boys Tad and Willie, joined by two playmates, took rags and old clothes and made a doll they named Jack. And they sentenced Jack to be shot at sunrise for sleeping on picket duty. They were burying Jack when the head gardener asked, "Why don't you have Jack pardoned?"

Into the White house chased the four boys, upstairs to a desk where the President dropped his work, heard them, and soberly wrote on a sheet of executive mansion stationery:

"The doll Jack is pardoned.
By order of the President.
A. Lincoln"

In a week, however, Jack was found hanging by the neck, dangling from a branch of a big bush in the garden, with Tad saying, "Jack was a traitor and a spy."

* * *

Press accounts told of an army surgeon who was court-martialed. His attorney brought the papers to Lincoln, who read the indictment of "drunkenness," commenting, "That's bad, very bad," and further along came to "insulting a lady." "That's bad, too. An officer shouldn't insult a lady, by any means. I'm afraid I can't reinstate this man."

On the attorney's request, Lincoln read further, regarding an attempt by the surgeon to kiss a lady. He scratched his head, looked up at the attorney, and said, "Really, I don't know about this. There are exceptions to every rule but as a general thing it's very hard to insult a lady by kissing her. But it seems the doctor only attempted to kiss her—perhaps the insult consisted in his not fully succeeding. I don't know as I ought to interfere in behalf of a man who attempts to kiss a lady and doesn't do it."

The attorney urged that a third party had made the complaint, with no evidence that the lady herself felt insulted. "That's a fact," said the President. "We can easily dispose of the kissing part. But I must look into the drunkenness a little. I can't overlook that. I'll have to get good evidence that it was strictly a New Year's offence, and is not a common occurrence with the Doctor."

POLITICIANS

On one bitter political enemy:

"I've been told that insanity is hereditary in his family, and I think we will admit the plea in his case."

❧   ❧   ❧

Speech in the U.S. House of Representatives
July 27, 1848:

"Have no fears, gentlemen, of your candidate; he exactly suits you, and we congratulate you upon it. However much you may be distressed about *our* candidate, you have all cause to be contented and happy with your own. If elected, he may not maintain all, or even any, of his positions previously taken; but he will be sure to do whatever the party exigency, for the time being, may require; and that is precisely what you want. He and Van Buren are the same 'manner of men'; and, like Van Buren, he will never desert *you* till you first desert *him*.

"Mr. Speaker, I adopt the suggestion of a friend, that General Cass is a general of splendidly successful *charges*—charges, to be sure, not upon the public enemy, but upon the public treasury."

❧   ❧   ❧

Lincoln made these comments about George Forquer, a political opponent who had accepted an appointment to a $3,000-a-year job, affording him the opportunity to build a home with a lightning rod, very unusual in those days.

"I desire to live, and I desire place and distinction; but I would rather die now than, like the gentleman, live to see the day that I could change my politics for an office worth $3,000 a year, and then feel compelled to erect a lightning rod to protect a guilty conscience from an offended God."

❧   ❧   ❧

104

One pest of a politician, who might be called So-and-So, came to Lincoln often asking offices, suggesting removals, and seeking creation of new offices. Lincoln, reviewing his day's routine to a friend, said that at night, as the closing act of the day, "I look under the bed to see if So-and-So is there, and if not, I thank heaven and bounce in."

✿ ✿ ✿

Late one Sunday afternoon Lincoln was telling his caller, Senator John B. Henderson of Missouri, that Charles Sumner and Senator Wilson, with Thaddeus Stevens, were constantly putting pressure on him to issue an emancipation proclamation. "They are coming and urging me, sometimes alone, sometimes in couples, sometimes all three together, but *constantly* pressing me." And with that Lincoln stepped to the window and, preposterously enough, Sumner, Wilson, and Stevens were coming toward the White House. Lincoln called to Henderson, pointed to the three approaching figures, and began telling of a school he went to when he was a boy in Indiana where the Bible was read out loud by the pupils. "One day we were standing up reading the account of the three Hebrew children in the fiery furnace. A little tow-headed fellow who stood beside me had the verse with the unpronounceable names. He mangled up Shadrach and Meshach woefully and finally went all to pieces on Abednego." For this the boy took a licking that made him cry. Then the class reading went on again, each boy in turn, till the same tow-headed boy was reached again. As he looked in the Bible and saw the verse he was to read, he let out a pitiful yell. The schoolmaster asked what was the matter. The boy, pointing to the next verse, cried out, "Look there! Look! There come them same damn three fellers again!"

POLITICS

"In politics, every man must skin his own skunk."

❀   ❀   ❀

To the Springfield Washington Temperance Society, 1842:

"When the conduct of men is designed to be influenced, *persuasion*, kind, unassuming persuasion, should ever be adopted. It is an old and true maxim, that a 'drop of honey catches more flies than a gallon of gall.' So with men. If you would win a man to your cause, *first* convince him that you are his sincere friend. Therein is a drop of honey that catches his heart, which, say what he will, is the great high road to his reason, and which, when once gained, you will find but little trouble in convincing his judgment of the justice of your cause, if indeed that cause really be a just one. On the contrary, assume to dictate to his judgment, or to command his action, or to mark him as one to be shunned and despised, and he will retreat within himself, close all the avenues to his head and his heart; and tho' your cause be naked truth itself . . . you shall no more be able to [reach] him, than to penetrate the hard shell of a tortoise with a rye straw.

"Such is man, and so *must* he be understood by those who would *lead* him, even to his own best interest."

❀   ❀   ❀

The 1848 campaign:

A recent speech by the Georgia representative (a learned man "so far as I could judge, not being learned myself") had struck him. The Georgian, Alfred Iverson, had charged the Whigs with abandoning Henry Clay. But, Lincoln answered, the Democrats had done the same to Martin Van Buren. Opponents charged the Taylor supporters with hiding under the gen-

106

eral's military coattail. But Jackson's had been long enough to cover five presidential races. "Like a horde of hungry ticks you have stuck to the tail of the Hermitage lion to the end of his life; and you are still sticking to it, and drawing loathsome sustenance from it, after he is dead."

      ✿   ✿   ✿

Lincoln conceded that this might not be the proper subject for a speech before Congress, but he wished "the gentlemen on the other side to understand, that the use of degrading figures is a game at which they may not find themselves able to take all the winnings." The only military tail Cass had was the one biographers attached to him. "He invaded Canada without resistance and outvaded it without pursuit." If there was some question about whether Cass broke his sword, threw it away, or what, it was "a fair historical compromise to say, if he did not break it, he did not do anything else with it."

      ✿   ✿   ✿

From a speech at Kalamazoo, Michigan
August 27, 1856:

"Fillmore, however, will go out of this contest the most national man we have. He has no prospect of having a single vote on either side of Mason and Dixon's line, to trouble his poor soul about."

      ✿   ✿   ✿

Shortly after his marriage to Mary Todd:

"It would astonish, if not amuse, the older citizens . . . who twelve years ago knew me a strange, friendless, uneducated, penniless boy, working on a flat boat at ten dollars per month, to learn that I have been put down here as the candidate of pride, wealth, and aristocratic family distinction."

      ✿   ✿   ✿

During the senatorial canvass, Lincoln and a young journalist waited together for a late train, seeking refuge from a thunderstorm in an empty freight car:

"My friends got me into *this* business. I did not consider myself qualified for the United States Senate, and it took me a long time to persuade myself that I was. . . . Mary insists, however, that I am going to be a senator and President of the United States, too. . . . Just think of such a sucker as me as President!"

❀ ❀ ❀

"Douglas introduced the Nebraska bill in January. In February afterwards, there was a call session of the Illinois legislature. Of the one hundred members composing the two branches of that body, about seventy were Democrats. These latter held a caucus, in which the Nebraska bill was talked of, if not formally discussed. It was thereby discovered that just three, and no more, were in favor of the measure. In a day or two Douglas' orders came on to have resolutions passed approving the bill; and they were passed by large majorities!!! The truth of this is vouched for by a bolting Democratic member. The masses, too, Democratic as well as Whig, were even nearer unanimous against it; but as soon as the party necessity of supporting it became apparent, the way the Democracy began to see the *wisdom* and *justice* of it, was perfectly astonishing."

❀ ❀ ❀

First Lincoln-Douglas debate, August 21, 1858:

"With public sentiment, nothing can fail; without it, nothing can succeed. Consequently he who molds public sentiment goes deeper than he who enacts statutes or pronounces decisions."

❀ ❀ ❀

Once he rode to a meeting with a Democratic candidate in a rig belonging to his opponent. At the meeting he told the farmers: "I am too poor to own a carriage, but my friend has generously invited me to ride with him. I want you to vote for me if you will; but, if not, then vote for my opponent, for he is a fine man."

✿ ✿ ✿

"Our policy, then, is to give no offense to others—leave them in a mood to come to us if they shall be compelled to give up their first love. This, too, is dealing justly with all, and leaving us in a mood to support heartily whoever shall be nominated."

✿ ✿ ✿

Douglas was reelected by a narrow margin.

"The fight must go on," Lincoln told a friend. "The cause of civil liberty must not be surrendered at the end of one or even one hundred defeats." Even so, it hurt. "I feel like the boy who stumped his toe," he said. "I am too big to cry and too badly hurt to laugh."

✿ ✿ ✿

"I have found that it is not entirely safe, when one is misrepresented under his very nose, to allow the misrepresentation to go uncontradicted."

(1859)

✿ ✿ ✿

"When a man hears himself somewhat misrepresented, it provokes him—at least, I find it so with myself; but when the misrepresentation becomes very gross and palpable, it is more apt to amuse him."

✿ ✿ ✿

A committee from the Ohio Legislature accompanied the President-elect on his ride to Columbus on the Little Miami

109

Railroad. A news writer on the train felt that Lincoln looked tired, and was resting himself, it seemed, by keeping up a steady flow of conversation. He touched on politics only once, saying that the demands of the South reminded him of his two boys, Tad and Willie, when they were smaller. One had a toy the other wanted and clamored for. At last, when the boy was told to let his brother have it in order to keep him quiet, he blurted, "No, sir, I must have it to quiet myself!"

❊   ❊   ❊

Cabinet members protesting the appointment of a Democrat, received the reply: "Oh, I can't afford to punish every person who has seen fit to oppose my election. We want a competent man in this office."

❊   ❊   ❊

"I cannot run the political machine. I have enough on my hands without that. It is the people's business—the election is in their hands. If they turn their backs to the fire, and get scorched in the rear, they'll find they have to sit on the blister."

(1864)

❊   ❊   ❊

A delegation called to present a paper reflecting discredit in the matter of appointments on Lincoln's old friend, Senator Baker. Lincoln took it in his hands, asking, "Is this paper mine to do with as I please?" The delegation replied, "Certainly, Mr. President." Lincoln laid the paper on live coals in the fireplace, watched it burn, and rose to say, "Good morning, gentlemen." When they had gone, he told Senator Henry Wilson: "They did not know what they were talking about when they made Ned Baker responsible for what I had done or proposed to do. They told me that that was my paper to do with as I liked. I could not trust myself to reply in words, I was so angry. That was the whole case."

110

POLICY AND PRINCIPLES

"Stand with anybody that stands *right*. Stand with him while he is right and *part* with him when he goes wrong."

❀   ❀   ❀

"If we could first know *where* we are, and *whither* we are tending, we could then better judge *what* to do, and *how* to do it."

❀   ❀   ❀

As a politician, Lincoln operated by a code of his own. An all-night session was held by the members of the legislature favoring Springfield for the state capital, and Lincoln was told of a block of votes he could have if he would give his vote for a measure that he considered against his principles; the members went home at daybreak without having brought him around to their way.

A second meeting was called; again they tried to ride down Lincoln's objections. Midnight came, the candles burned low, all were tired. Lincoln began speaking amid silence, seriously and with feeling, telling why he couldn't in such a case trade his vote.

"You may burn my body to ashes, and scatter them to the winds of heaven; you may drag my soul down to the regions of darkness and despair to be tormented forever; but you will never get me to support a measure which I believe to be wrong, although by doing so I may accomplish that which I believe to be right."

❀   ❀   ❀

"My oath . . . imposed upon me the duty of preserving, by every indispensable means, that government—that nation—of which that Constitution was the organic law. Was it possible to lose the nation, and yet preserve the Constitution? By general

111

law life and limb must be protected; yet often a limb must be amputated to save a life; but a life is never wisely given to save a limb. I felt that measures, otherwise unconstitutional, might become lawful, by becoming indispensable to the preservation of the Constitution, through the preservation of the nation."

✿ ✿ ✿

Cooper Institute, February 27, 1860:

"Neither let us be slandered from our duty by false accusations against us, nor frightened from it by menaces of destruction to the government, nor of dungeons to ourselves. Let us have faith that right makes might, and in that faith let us to the end dare to do our duty as we understand it."

✿ ✿ ✿

To Horace Greeley
August 22, 1862:

As to the policy I "seem to be pursuing" as you say, I have not meant to leave any one in doubt.

I would save the Union. I would save it the shortest way under the Constitution. The sooner the national authority can be restored; the nearer the Union will be "the Union as it was." If there be those who would not save the Union, unless they could at the same time *save* slavery, I do not agree with them. If there be those who would not save the Union unless they could at the same time *destroy* slavery, I do not agree with them. My paramount object in this struggle *is* to save the Union, and is *not* either to save or to destroy slavery. If I could save the Union without freeing *any* slave I would do it, and if I could save it by freeing *all* the slaves I would do it; and if I could save it by freeing some and leaving others alone I would also do that. What I do about slavery, and the colored race, I do because I believe it helps to save the Union; and what I forbear, I forbear because I do *not* believe it would help to save the Union. I shall do *less* whenever I shall believe what I am doing hurts the cause, and I shall do *more* whenever I shall believe doing more will help the cause. I shall try to correct errors when shown to be errors; and I shall adopt new views so fast as they shall appear to be true views.

❖ ❖ ❖

"I have here stated my purpose according to my view of *official* duty; and I intend no modification of my oft-expressed personal wish that all men everywhere could be free."

❖ ❖ ❖

To illustrate a shifting political policy, Lincoln told the story of a farm boy whose father instructed him in plowing a new furrow: "Steer for that yoke of oxen standing at the farther end of the field." The father went away, and the boy followed instructions. But the oxen began moving. The boy followed them around the field, and furrowed a circle instead of a line!

❖ ❖ ❖

John M. Palmer, the Union Democrat of Illinois, waited in a White House anteroom one morning until he was told to enter the President's office. As Palmer told it, he found Lincoln in the hands of the barber, and Lincoln called: "Come in, Palmer, come in. You're home folks. I can shave before you. I couldn't before those others and I have to do it sometime." They chatted and Palmer finally spoke in a frank and jovial manner. "Mr. Lincoln, if anybody had told me that in a great crisis like this the people were going out to a little one-horse town and pick out a one-horse lawyer for President I wouldn't have believed it." Lincoln leaned forward, put a hand on Palmer's knee, and said: "Neither would I. But it was a time when a man with a policy would have been fatal to the country. I have never had a policy. I have simply tried to do what seemed best as each day came."

❖ ❖ ❖

"There are men in Congress who possess feelings of hate and vindictiveness in which I do not sympathize and can not participate."

✿ ✿ ✿

From a speech at Clinton, Illinois, September 8, 1858:

"If you once forfeit the confidence of your fellow citizens, you can never regain their respect and esteem. It is true that you may fool all of the people some of the time; you can even fool some of the people all of the time; but you can't fool all of the people all of the time."

THE PRESIDENCY

To an office seeker:

There are no emoluments that properly belong to patriotism. I brought nothing with me to the White House, nor am I likely to carry anything out.

*　*　*

In a letter to Herndon, Lincoln explained that the President of the United States is the same as a king, in power, if he can do what President Polk had done in commencing the Mexican War:

Allow the President to invade a neighboring nation whenever he shall deem it necessary to repel an invasion, and you allow him to do so whenever he may choose to say he deems it necessary for such purpose, and you allow him to make war at pleasure. Study to see if you can fix any limit to his power in this respect. If today he should choose to say he thinks it necessary to invade Canada to prevent the British from invading us, how could you stop him? You may say to him, "I see no probability of the British invading us;" but he will say to you, "Be silent: I see it, if you don't."

*　*　*

T.J. Pickett, Esq.
April 16, 1859:

My Dear Sir:
Yours of the 13th, is just received. My engagements are such that I cannot, at any very early day, visit Rock Island, to deliver a lecture, or for any other object.
As to the matter you kindly mention, I must, in candor, say I do not think myself fit for the Presidency. I certainly am flattered, and gratified, that some partial friends think of me in that connection; but I really think it best for our cause that no concerted effort, such as you suggest, should be made.

Let this be considered confidential.

Yours very truly,

✿ ✿ ✿

A young man argued that Millard Fillmore ought to be elected President because he was such a "good" man. Lincoln had known this lad for years, and he said: "My young friend, I think you are making a mistake in voting for Mr. Fillmore because of his goodness. You can do something so much better. There is One whose goodness and greatness all agree far exceed Mr. Fillmore's and, in fact, all others that could be named. No one will question this; no one doubts it. So on the 6th of next November I advise you to go the polls and vote for Almighty God for President. He is unquestionably the best being that exists. There is practically as much chance of electing God Almighty President of the United States at this time, as Millard Fillmore."

✿ ✿ ✿

When he heard the news of his nomination in the Springfield office of his longtime newspaper supporter, the *Illinois State Journal*, Lincoln said: "Gentlemen, you had better come up and shake my hand while you can. Honors elevate some men, you know."

✿ ✿ ✿

To an Ohio committee requesting suspension of the draft until after the elections, Lincoln answered "What is the Presidency worth to me if I have no country?"

✿ ✿ ✿

Not long after his second inauguration, Lincoln confided to Treasury Secretary McCulloch: "I am here by the blunders of the Democrats. If instead of resolving that the war was a failure, they had resolved that I was a failure and denounced me for not more vigorously prosecuting it, I should not have been reelected."

✿ ✿ ✿

116

After one cabinet meeting in March, young Fred Seward heard Postmaster General Dennison say of the little old leather-covered chair at Lincoln's desk, "I should think the Presidential chair of the United States might be a better piece of furniture than that." Lincoln turned, let his eyes scan the worn, torn, battered leather. "You think that's not a good chair, Governor?" and with a half-quizzical, half-meditative look at it: "There are a great many people that want to sit in it, though. I'm sure I've often wished some of them had it instead of me!"

✿ ✿ ✿

August 23, 1864:

"This morning, as for some days past, it seems exceedingly probable that this administration will not be reelected. Then it will be my duty to so co-operate with the President-elect, as to save the Union between the election and the inauguration; as he will have secured his election on such ground that he cannot possibly save it afterwards."

POETRY AND PUNS

An early poem:

> The very spot where grew the bread
>> That formed my bones, I see.
> How strange, old field, on thee to tread
>> And feel I'm part of thee.

✿   ✿   ✿

> Time! what an empty vapor 'tis!
>> And days how swift they are:
> Swift as an Indian arrow—
>> Fly on like a shooting star,
> The present moment just is here,
>> Then slides away in haste,
> That we can never say they're ours,
>> But only say they're past.

✿   ✿   ✿

For the wedding of his sister Sarah to Aaron Grigsby, he wrote Adam and Eve's Wedding Song. The final three verses read:

> The woman was not taken
>> From Adam's feet, we see,
> So he must not abuse her,
>> The meaning seems to be.

> The woman was not taken
>> From Adam's head, we know,
> To show she must not rule him—
>> Tis evidently so.

> The woman she was taken
>> From under Adam's arm,

So she must be protected
From injuries and harm.

✿　✿　✿

September 28, 1858

Notes to daughters of innkeeper at Winchester, Illinois:

To Rosa:

You are young, and I am older;
You are hopeful, I am not—
Enjoy life, ere it grow colder—
Pluck the roses ere they rot.

Teach your beau to heed the lay—
That sunshine soon is lost in shade—
That *now's* as good as any day—
To take thee, Rosa, ere she fade.

To Linnie:

A sweet plaintive song did I hear,
And I fancied that she was the singer—
May emotions as pure, as that song set astir
Be the worst that the future shall bring her.

✿　✿　✿

Whatever spiteful fools may say,
Each jealous ranting yelper,
No woman ever went astray,
Without a man to help her.

✿　✿　✿

Epitaph for Kickapoo Indian Johnny Kongapod:

> Here lies poor Johnny Kongapod;
> Have mercy on him, gracious God.
> As he would do if he was God
>   And you were Johnny Kongapod.

❋   ❋   ❋

> Fondly do we hope—
>   fervently do we pray—
> that this mighty scourge of war
>   may speedily pass away.

RECONSTRUCTION

Second Inaugural Address
March 4, 1865:

"With malice toward none; with charity for all; with firmness in the right, as God gives us to see the right, let us strive on to finish the work we are in; to bind up the nation's wounds; to care for him who shall have borne the battle, and for his widow, and his orphan—to do all which may achieve and cherish a just, and a lasting peace, among ourselves, and with all nations."

✿　✿　✿

July 26, 1862
Hon. Reverdy Johnson
My Dear Sir:

Yours of the 16th by the hand of Governor Shepley is received. It seems the Union feeling in Louisiana is being crushed out by the course of General Phelps. Please pardon me for believing that is a false pretense. The people of Louisiana—all intelligent people everywhere—know full well, that I never had a wish to touch the foundations of their society, or any right of theirs. With perfect knowledge of this, they forced a necessity upon me to send armies among them, and it is their own fault, not mine, that they are annoyed by the presence of General Phelps. They also know the remedy—know how to be cured of General Phelps. Remove the necessity of his presence. . . .

✿　✿　✿

"Concede that the new government of Louisiana is only to what it should be as the egg is to the fowl, we shall sooner have the fowl by hatching the egg than by smashing it."

✿ ✿ ✿

To Edwin M. Stanton
February 5, 1864:

Submitted to the Sec. of War. On principle I dislike an oath which requires a man to swear he *has* not done wrong. It rejects the Christian principle of forgiveness on terms of repentance. I think it is enough if the man does no wrong *hereafter*."

✿ ✿ ✿

To Ulysses S. Grant:

August 14, 1864
Lieut. Genl. Grant
City-Point, Va.

The Secretary of War and I concur that you better confer with Gen. Lee and stipulate for a mutual discontinuance of house-burning and other destruction of private property. The time and manner of conference, and particulars of stipulation we leave, on our part, to your convenience and judgment.

✿ ✿ ✿

Newspaper correspondent Charles Carleton Coffin was at headquarters and Lincoln greeted him: "What news have you?"
"I have just arrived from Charleston and Savannah."
"Indeed! Well, I'm right glad to see you. How do the people like being back in the Union again?"
"I think some of them are reconciled to it, if we may draw conclusions from the action of one planter, who, while I was there, came down the Savannah River with his whole family—

wife, children, Negro woman and her children, of whom he was father—and with his crop of cotton which he was anxious to sell at the highest price."

"Oh, yes, I see." Lincoln brightened. "I see, patriarchal times once more; Abraham, Sarah, Isaac, Hagar and Ishmael, all in one boat!" And with a chuckle: "I reckon they'll accept the situation now that they can sell their cotton."

       ❉   ❉   ❉

Regarding the Confederate officials: "Frighten them out of the country," he urged, "open the gates, let down the bars, scare them off!"

General William Tecumseh Sherman once asked Lincoln explicitly whether he wanted Jefferson Davis captured or allowed to escape. Lincoln replied:

"I'll tell you, General, what I think of taking Jeff Davis. Out in Illinois there was an old temperance lecturer who was very strict in the doctrine and practice of total abstinence. One day, after a long ride in the hot sun, he stopped at the house of a friend, who proposed making him a lemonade. When the friend asked if he wouldn't like a drop of something stronger in the drink, he replied that he couldn't think of it. 'I'm opposed to it on principle,' he said. 'But,' he added with a longing glance at the bottle conveniently at hand, 'if you could manage to put in a drop unbeknownst to me, I guess it wouldn't hurt me much.' Now, General, I am bound to oppose the escape of Jeff Davis; but if you could manage to let him slip out *unbeknownst-like*, I guess it wouldn't hurt me much."

RELIGION

"If the church would ask simply for assent to the Savior's statement of the substance of the law: 'Thou shalt love the lord thy God with all thy heart, and with all thy soul, and with all thy mind, and they neighbor as thyself'—that church would I gladly unite with."

✿ ✿ ✿

What Lincoln had of mystic faith and inner outlook was hidden. "I am very sure," he once said to Noah Brooks, "that if I do not go away from here a wiser man, I shall go away a better man, for having learned here what a very poor sort of a man I am."

✿ ✿ ✿

After Lincoln's reelection he made a speech from a White House window saying he had no sense of personal triumph but gave "thanks to the Almighty for this evidence of the people's resolution to stand by free government and the rights of humanity."

✿ ✿ ✿

Meditation on the Divine Will
circa early September 1862:

The will of God prevails. In great contest each party claims to act in accordance with the will of God. Both *may* be, and one *must* be wrong. God can not be *for*, and *against* the same thing at the same time. In the present civil war it is quite possible that God's purpose is something different from the purpose of either party—and yet the human instrumentalities, working just as they do, are of the best adaptation to effect His purpose. I am almost ready to say this is probably true—

that God wills this contest, and wills that it shall not end yet. By his mere quiet power, on the minds of the new contestants, he could have either *saved* or *destroyed* the Union without a human contest. Yet the contest began. And having begun, He could give the final victory to either side any day. Yet the contest proceeds.

✿   ✿   ✿

When a California man told Lincoln about an old Springfield storyteller he had met on the West Coast, Lincoln was reminded that the former Illinois man, a dry wit, had once been State Secretary, and a meek cadaverous stranger entered the office one day requesting a permit for a room in the Capitol to deliver lectures. "May I ask what is to be the subject of your lectures?" "Certainly. The course I wish to deliver is on the Second Coming of Our Lord." "It is of no use. If you will take my advice, you will not waste your time in this city. It is my private opinion that if the Lord has been in Springfield once He will never come the second time."

✿   ✿   ✿

From the *Charleston Mercury* in 1864:

A minister in line with a delegation meeting the President "hoped the Lord is on our side." The President: "I don't agree with you." There was amazement. He continued: "I am not at all concerned about that, for we know that the Lord is always on the side of the right. But it is my constant anxiety and prayer that I and this nation should be on the Lord's side."

✿   ✿   ✿

"Pa," demanded Tad, "why do the preachers always pray so long for you?" The father's smile faded. "I suppose," he said, "it's because the preachers think I need it," and half to himself, "I guess I do."

✿   ✿   ✿

125

December 6, 1864:

On Thursday of the week before, two ladies from Tennessee came before the President asking the release of their husbands held as prisoners of war at Johnson's Island. They were put off till Friday, when they came again; and were again put off to Saturday. At each of the interviews one of the ladies argued that her husband was a religious man. On Saturday the President ordered the release of the prisoners, and then said to the lady, "You say your husband is a religious man; tell him when you meet him, that I say I am not much of a judge of religion, but that, in my opinion, the religion that sets men to rebel and fight against their government because, as they think, that government does not sufficiently help *some* men to eat their bread on the sweat of *other* men's faces, is not the sort of religion upon which people can get to heaven!"

✿   ✿   ✿

Lincoln's storytelling was so legendary that tales started circulating about him. One he was fond of telling on himself was about two Quaker women overheard in conversation:

"I think Jefferson will succeed," said the first.
"Why dost thee think so?" asked the second.
"Because Jefferson is a praying man."
"And so is Abraham a praying man."
"Yes, but the Lord will think Abraham is joking."

✿   ✿   ✿

Lincoln queried a group of Chicago ministers who were urging immediate and universal emancipation: "Now, gentlemen, if I cannot enforce the Constitution down South, how am I to enforce a mere Presidential proclamation?"

He assured them he was trying to find his path through a diversity of beliefs. "I am approached with the most opposite opinions and advice, and by religious men certain that they represent the divine will. I hope it will not be irreverent for me to say that if it is probable that God would reveal his will to others, on a point so connected with my duty, it might be supposed he would reveal it directly to me. And if I can learn what it is, I will do it. These are not, however, the days of miracles, and I suppose I am not to expect a direct revelation. I must study the plain, physical facts of the case . . . and learn what appears to be wise and right. Do not misunderstand me because I have mentioned these objections. They indicate the difficulties . . . the subject is on my mind by day and night. Whatever shall appear to be God's will, I will do."

       ✿   ✿   ✿

One story John Nicolay heard Lincoln tell had as its central character a hard-working backwoods housewife in her log cabin, with many children running around, the typical pioneer struggling to make "the best of things." A wandering Methodist preacher appeared and tried to sell her a Bible. She was polite to begin with, but she didn't like the way he pushed some questions. Shouldn't every home have a Bible? Did she have a Bible in this home? Her sharp answer was that of course they owned a Bible. If so, where was it? the man asked. She began a search, but found no Bible. She called the children and they joined in the hunt for the missing Bible. At last one of them dug up from some corner and held up in triumph a few torn and ragged pages of Holy Writ. The man argued that it was not a proper Bible, and how could they pretend it was? The woman stuck to her claim. Of course they had a Bible in the house, "But I had no idea we were so nearly out!"

THE SECESSIONIST SOUTH

Lincoln describes the hostile sections the nation had fallen into by 1854:

"The South, flushed with triumph and tempted to excesses; the North, betrayed, as they believe, brooding on wrong and burning for revenge. One side will provoke, the other resent. The one will taunt, the other defy; one aggresses, the other retaliates."

✿　✿　✿

Address at Cooper Institute, New York City
February 27, 1860:

"Under all these circumstances, do you really feel yourselves justified to break up this government unless such a court decision as yours is, shall be at once submitted to as a conclusive and final rule of political action? But you will not abide the election of a Republican president! In that supposed event, you say, you will destroy the Union; and then, you say, the great crime of having destroyed it will be upon us! That is cool. A highwayman holds a pistol to my ear, and mutters through his teeth, 'Stand and deliver, or I shall kill you, and then you will be a murderer!'

"To be sure, what the robber demanded of me—my money—was my own; and I had a clear right to keep it; but it was no more my own than my vote is my own; and the threat of death to me, to extort my money, and the threat of destruction to the Union, to extort my vote, can scarcely be distinguished in principle."

✿　✿　✿

From the first inaugural address:

"I am loth to close. We are not enemies, but friends. We must not be enemies. Though passion may have strained, it

128

must not break our bonds of affection. The mystic chords of memory, stretching from every battlefield and patriot grave, to every living heart and hearthstone, all over this broad land, will yet swell the chorus of the Union, when again touched, as surely they will be, by the better angels of our nature."

✿ ✿ ✿

"If one State may secede, so may another; and when all shall have seceded, none is left to pay the debts. Is this quite just to creditors? Did we notify them of this sage view of ours when we borrowed their money? If we now recognize this doctrine by allowing the seceders to go in peace, it is difficult to see what we can do if others choose to go or to extort terms upon which they will promise to remain.

"To be consistent they must secede from one another whenever they shall find it the easiest way to settling their debts, or effecting any other selfish or unjust object."

✿ ✿ ✿

Inauguration speech:

"In your hands my dissatisfied countrymen, and not in mine, is the momentous issue of civil war. The government will not assail you. You can have no conflict, without being yourselves the aggressors. You have no oath registered in Heaven to destroy the government, while I shall have the most solemn one to 'preserve, protect and defend' it."

✿ ✿ ✿

To Senate & House of Representatives
July 4, 1861:

"The seceders insist that our Constitution admits of secession. They have assumed to make a national constitution of their own, in which, of necessity, they have either *discarded*, or *retained*, the right of secession, as they insist, it exists in ours. If

129

they have discarded it, they thereby admit that, on principle, it ought not to be ours. If they have retained it, by their own construction of ours they show that to be consistent they must secede from one another, whenever they shall find it the easiest way of settling their debts, or effecting any other selfish or unjust object. The principle itself is one of disintegration, and upon which no government can possibly endure . . ."

❈ ❈ ❈

First inaugural address:

"Plainly, the central idea of secession, is the essence of anarchy. A majority, held in restraint by constitutional checks, and limitations, and always changing easily, with deliberate changes of popular opinions and sentiments, is the only true sovereign of a free people. Whoever rejects it, does, of necessity, fly to anarchy or to despotism. Unanimity is impossible; the rule of a minority, as a permanent arrangement, is wholly inadmissible; so that, rejecting the majority principle, anarchy, or despotism in some form, is all that is left."

❈ ❈ ❈

From the Marquis de Chambrun, who had come to the *River Queen* as Lincoln's guest on April 6:

He then asked me if I had ever heard "Dixie" . . . As I answered in the negative, he added: "That tune is now Federal property; it belongs to us, and at any rate, it is good to show the rebels that with us they will be free to hear it again." He then ordered the somewhat surprised musicians to play it.

❈ ❈ ❈

When his eldest son, Robert, showed him a picture of General Robert E. Lee, the Presidennt looked at it thoughtfully and said: "It is a good face; it is the face of a noble, noble, brave man. I am glad that the war is over at last."

SLAVERY

"If slavery is not wrong, nothing is wrong. I cannot remember when I did not so think, and feel."

✿ ✿ ✿

"No man is good enough to govern another man without that other's consent. Familiarize yourselves with the chains of bondage and you prepare your own limbs to wear them."

(1854)

✿ ✿ ✿

On meeting Ward Hill Lamon (1847), a young Virginian destined to become a close friend:

"Oh, yes, you Virginians shed barrels of perspiration while standing off at a distance and superintending the work your slaves do for you. . . . Here it is every fellow for himself, or he doesn't get there."

✿ ✿ ✿

"As I would not be a slave, so I would not be a master. This expresses my idea of democracy. Whatever differs from this, to the extent of the difference, is not democracy."

✿ ✿ ✿

Fragment on Slavery (1854):

If A can prove, however conclusively, that he may, of right, enslave B—why may not B snatch the same argument, and prove equally, that he may enslave A?

You say A is white, and B is black. It is *color*, then; the lighter having the right to enslave the darker? Take care. By this rule, you are to be slave to the first man you meet with a fairer skin than your own.

You do not mean *color* exactly?—You mean the whites are

intellectually the superiors of the blacks, and, therefore have the right to enslave them? Take care again.

By this rule, you are to be slave to the first man you meet with an intellect superior to your own.

But, say you, it is a question of *interest*; and, if you can make it your *interest*, you have the right to enslave another. Very well. And if he can make it his interest, he has the right to enslave you.

❁ ❁ ❁

"What I do say is, that no man is good enough to govern another man, *without that other's consent*. I say this is the leading principle—the sheet anchor of American republicanism."

❁ ❁ ❁

September 11, 1854, regarding the Kansas-Nebraska law:

"The state of the case in a few words, is this: The Missouri Compromise excluded slavery from the Kansas-Nebraska territory. The repeal opened the territories to slavery. If there is any meaning to the declaration in the 14th section, that it does not mean to legislate slavery into the territories, it is this: that it does not require slaves to be sent there. The Kansas and Nebraska territories are now as open to slavery as Mississippi or Arkansas were when they were territories.

"To illustrate the case: Abraham Lincoln has a fine meadow, containing beautiful springs of water, and well fenced, which John Calhoun had agreed with Abraham (originally owning the land in common) should be his, and the agreement had been consummated in the most solemn manner, regarded by both as sacred. John Calhoun, however, in the course of time, had become owner of an extensive herd of cattle—the prairie grass had become dried up and there was no convenient water to be had. John Calhoun then looks with a longing eye on Lincoln's meadow, and goes to it and throws down the fences, and exposes it to the ravages of his starving and famishing cattle.

'You rascal,' says Lincoln, 'what have you done? What do you do this for?' 'Oh,' replies Calhoun, 'everything is right, I have taken down your fence; but nothing more. It is my true intent and meaning not to drive my cattle into your meadow, nor to exclude them therefrom, but to leave them perfectly free to form their own notions of the feed, and to direct their movements in their own way!'

"Now would not the man who committed this outrage be deemed both a knave and a fool—a knave in removing the restrictive fence, which he had solemnly pledged himself to sustain—and a fool in supposing that there could be one man found in the country to believe that he had not pulled down the fence for the purpose of opening the meadow for his cattle?"

❋   ❋   ❋

From a speech on the Kansas-Nebraska Act at Peoria, Illinois (quotes from Declaration of Independence):

"I have quoted so much at this time merely to show that according to our ancient faith, the just powers of governments are derived from the consent of the governed. Now the relation of masters and slaves is, *pro tanto*, a total violation of this principle. The master not only governs the slave without his consent; but he governs him by a set of rules altogether different from those which he prescribes for himself. Allow *all* the governed an equal voice in the government, and that, and that only, is self government."

More on the Kansas-Nebraska Act (speech at Peoria, Illinois):

"I particularly object to the *new* position which the avowed principle of this Nebraska law gives to slavery in the body politic. I object to it because it assumes that there *can* be *moral right* in the enslaving of one man by another. I object to it as a dangerous dalliance for a free people—a sad evidence that, seeking prosperity we forget right—that liberty, as a principle, we have ceased to revere."

❊   ❊   ❊

To Joshua F. Speed
August 24, 1855:

You say if Kansas fairly votes herself a free state, as a Christian you will rather rejoice at it. All decent slave-holders *talk* that way; and I do not doubt their candor. But they never *vote* that way. Although in a private letter, or conversation, you will express your preference that Kansas shall be free, you would vote for no man for Congress who would say the same thing publicly.

❊   ❊   ❊

Address at Cooper Institute, New York:

"Nor can we justifiably withhold this, on any ground save our conviction that slavery is wrong. If slavery is right, all words, acts, laws, and constitutions against it, are themselves wrong, and should be silenced, and swept away. If it is right, we cannot justly object to its nationality—its universality; if it is wrong, they cannot justly insist upon its extension—its enlargement. All they ask, we could readily grant, if we thought slavery right; all we ask, they could as readily grant, if they thought it wrong. Their thinking it right, and our thinking it wrong, is the precise fact upon which depends the whole controversy. Thinking it right, as they do, they are not to blame for desiring its full recognition, as being right; but, thinking it wrong, as we do, can we yield to them? Can we cast our votes with their view, and against our own? In view of our moral, social, and political responsibilities, can we do this?"

❊   ❊   ❊

From the sixth Lincoln-Douglas Debate, Quincy, Illinois:

134

"We have in this nation this element of domestic slavery. It is a matter of absolute certainty that it is a disturbing element. It is the opinion of all the great men who have expressed an opinion upon it, that it is a dangerous element. We keep up a controversy in regard to it. That controversy necessarily springs from difference of opinion, and if we can learn exactly—can reduce to the lowest elements—what that difference of opinion is, we perhaps shall be better prepared for discussing the different systems of policy that we would propose in regard to that disturbing element. I suggest that the difference of opinion, reduced to its lowest terms, is no other than the difference between the men who think slavery a wrong and those who do not think it wrong. The Republican party think it wrong—we think it is a moral, a social and a political wrong. We think it is a wrong not confining itself merely to the persons or the states where it exists, but that it is a wrong in its tendency, to say the least, that extends itself to the existence of the whole nation. Because we think it wrong, we proposed a course of policy that shall deal with it as a wrong. We deal with it as with any other wrong, in so far as we can prevent its growing any larger, and so deal with it that in the run of time there may be some promise of an end to it. . . .

"He [Judge Douglas] has the high distinction, so far as I know, of never having said slavery is either right or wrong. Almost everybody else says one or the other, but the Judge never does. If there be a man in the Democratic party who thinks it is wrong, and yet clings to that party, I suggest to him in the first place that his leader don't talk as he does, for he never says that it is wrong. In the second place, I suggest to him that if he will examine the policy proposed to be carried forward, he will find that he carefully excludes the idea that there is anything wrong in it. If you will examine the arguments that are made on it, you will find that every one carefully excludes the idea that there is anything wrong in slavery. Perhaps that Democrat who says he is as much opposed to slavery as I am, will tell me that I am wrong about this. I wish him to examine his own course in regard to this matter a moment, and then see if his opinion will not be changed a little. You say it is wrong; but don't you constantly object to anybody else saying so? Do you not constantly argue that this is not the right place to oppose it? You say it must not be opposed in the free states, because slavery is not here; it must not be opposed in the slave states, because it is there; it must not be opposed in politics, because that will make a fuss; it must not be opposed in the pulpit, because it is not religion. Then where is the place to oppose it? There is no suitable place to oppose it. There is no place in the country to oppose this evil overspreading the continent, which you say yourself is coming."

✥   ✥   ✥

From the Lincoln-Douglas debates:

Pointing to the Supreme Court decision that slaves as property could not be voted out of new territories, Lincoln said:

"His Supreme Court, cooperating with him, has squatted his squatter sovereignty out." The argument had got down as thin as "soup made by boiling the shadow of a pigeon that had starved to death."

✥   ✥   ✥

From a letter to Henry L. Pierce and others
Springfield, Illinois, April 6, 1959:

This is a world of compensations; and he who would *be* no slave, must consent to *have* no slave. Those who deny freedom to others, deserve it not for themselves; and, under a just God, can not long retain it.

✥   ✥   ✥

Why was slavery not mentioned in the U.S. Constitution. Why were the words Negro and slavery left out?

136

"It was hoped when it should be read by intelligent and patriotic men, after the institution of slavery had passed from among us, there should be nothing on the face of the great charter of liberty suggesting that such a thing as negro slavery had ever existed among us. They expected and intended that it should be put in the course of ultimate extinction."

✿　✿　✿

"Whenever I hear anyone arguing for slavery, I feel a strong impulse to see it tried on him personally."

✿　✿　✿

"Public discussion is helping to doom slavery. What kills a skunk is the publicity it gives itself."

✿　✿　✿

"This government was instituted to secure the blessings of freedom. Slavery is an unqualified evil to the Negro, to the white man, to the soil, and to the State."

✿　✿　✿

"A house divided against itself cannot stand. I believe this government cannot endure, permanently half slave and half free. I do not expect the Union to be dissolved—I do not expect the house to fall—but I do expect it will cease to be divided. It will become all one thing or all the other. Either the opponents of slavery will arrest the further spread of it, and place it where the public mind shall rest in the belief that it is in course of ultimate extinction; or its advocates will push it forward, till it shall become alike lawful in all the states, old as well as new—North as well as South. Have we no tendency to the latter condition?"

✿　✿　✿

Annual address to Congress, December 1, 1863:

"Fellow citizens, we cannot escape history. We of this Congress and this administration, will be remembered in spite of ourselves . . . In *giving* freedom to the *slave*, we *assure* freedom to the *free*—honorable alike in what we give, and what we preserve."

❈   ❈   ❈

"It may seem strange that any men should dare ask God's assistance in wringing their bread from the sweat of other men's faces, but let us judge not that we be not judged."

(1865)

❈   ❈   ❈

Speech at Edwardsville, Illinois:

"When by all these means you have succeeded in dehumanizing the Negro; when you have put him down and made it impossible for him to be but as the beasts of the field; when you have extinguished his soul, and placed him where the ray of hope is blown out in darkness that broods over the damned, are you quite sure the demon you have roused will not turn and rend you? What constitutes the bulwark of our liberty and independence? It is not our frowning battlements, our bristling seacoasts, the guns of our war steamers, or the strength of our gallant army. These are not our reliance against a resumption of tyranny in our land. All of them may be turned against our liberties without making us stronger or weaker for the struggle.

"Our reliance is in the love of liberty which God has planted in our bosoms. Our defense is in the preservation of the spirit which prizes liberty as the heritage of *all men, in all lands everywhere.* Destroy this spirit and you have planted the seeds of despotism around your own doors. Familiarize yourself with the chains of bondage, and you are preparing your own limbs to wear them.

"Accustomed to trample on the rights of those around you, you have lost the genius of your own independence, and

138

become the fit subjects of the first cunning tyrant who rises among you. And let me tell you that these things are prepared for you with the logic of history, if the elections shall promise that the next Dred Scott decision and all future decisions shall be acquiesced in by the people."

❖ ❖ ❖

Although determined to oppose the spread of slavery, Lincoln admitted that he did not know what to do about those states where it was already established and protected by a complex web of state and national laws.

"I have no prejudice against the Southern people. They are just what we would be in their situation. If slavery did not now exist amongst them, they would not introduce it. If it did now exist amongst us, we should not instantly give it up. . . . I surely will not blame them for not doing what I should not know how to do myself. If all earthly power were given me, I should not know what to do, as to the existing institution."

❖ ❖ ❖

A letter of April 1864 to Mrs. Horace Mann, widow of the famous educator who had been a fellow member in the 1848 Congress:

The petition of persons under eighteen, praying that I would free all slave children, and the heading of which petition it appears you wrote, was handed me a few days since by Senator Sumner. Please tell these little people I am very glad their young hearts are so full of just and generous sympathy, and that, while I have not the power to grant all they ask, I trust they will remember that God has, and that, as it seems, he wills to do it.

THE SOLDIERS

Message to Congress in Special Session:

"It is worthy of note, that while in this, the government's hour of trial, large numbers of those in the Army and Navy, who have been favored with the offices, have resigned, and proved false to the hand which had pampered them, not one common soldier, or common sailor is known to have deserted his flag."

✿   ✿   ✿

Advice to George Pickett, who was heading east to be a cadet at West Point:

"Deceit and falsehood, especially if you have got a bad memory, is the *worst* enemy a fellow can have.

"Now, boy, on your march, don't you go and forget the old maxim that 'one drop of honey catches more flies than a half-gallon of gall.' Load your musket with this maxim, and smoke it in your pipe."

✿   ✿   ✿

Four New York soldiers who were plumbers stacked arms in the White House kitchen and began a repair job. The Commander-in-Chief entered, sat down and chuckled: "Boys, I certainly am glad to see you. I hope you can fix that thing right off, for if you can't, the cook can't use the range and I don't suppose I'll get any grub today."

✿   ✿   ✿

A young German count, vouched for by the Prussian legation as of noble blood, seeking a place in the army, was introduced to Lincoln by Carl Schurz. The count assured Lincoln that his family stood high; they had been counts for centuries.

140

"Well," said Lincoln, "that need not trouble you. That will not be in your way, if you behave yourself as a soldier." The young count was puzzled and asked Schurz, as they walked away, what in the world the President could have meant by so strange a remark.

✿ ✿ ✿

To Edwin M. Stanton
March 1, 1864:

My dear Sir:
A poor widow, by the name of Baird, has a son in the Army, that for some offence has been sentenced to serve a long time without pay, or at most, with very little pay. I do not like this punishment of withholding pay—it falls so hard upon poor families. After he has been serving in this way for several months, at the tearful appeal of the poor Mother, I made a direction that he be allowed to enlist for a new term, on the same conditions as others. She now comes, and says she can not get it acted upon. Please do it. Yours truly.

✿ ✿ ✿

July 15, 1862
Hon. Sec. of War
My dear Sir:
This young man—George K. Pomroy—is the son of one of the best women I ever knew—a widow who has lost all her other children, and has cheerfully given this one to the war, and devotes herself exclusively to nursing our sick and wounded soldiers. I wish to do something for him, and even, to strain a point for that object. I wish you would see him, and give him a second lieutenancy in the regular army, in the first vacancy not already promised. He has already served nearly a year in the volunteers. This shall be your voucher. Yours truly,"

✿ ✿ ✿

141

To the 166th Ohio Regiment
August 22, 1864:

"I suppose you are going home to see your families and friends. For the service you have done in this great struggle in which we are engaged I present you sincere thanks for myself and the country. I almost always feel inclined, when I happen to say anything to soldiers, to impress upon them in a few brief remarks the importance of success in this contest. It is not merely for today, but for all time to come that we should perpetuate for our children's children this great and free government, which we have enjoyed all our lives. I beg you to remember this, not merely for my sake, but for yours. I happen temporarily to occupy this big White House. I am a living witness that any one of your children may look to come here as my father's child has. It is in order that each of you may have through this free government which we have enjoyed, an open field and a fair chance for your industry, enterprise and intelligence; that you may all have equal privileges in the race of life, with all its desirable human aspirations. It is for this the struggle should be maintained, that we may not lose our birthright—not only for one, but for two or three years. The nation is worth fighting for, to secure such an inestimable jewel."

*　*　*

Reluctant to approve the death penalty, he spoke to a visitor to his office.

"Do you see those papers crowded in those pigeonholes [in my desk]? They are the cases you call by that long title, 'cowardice in the face of the enemy.' I call them, for short, my 'leg cases.' I put it to you, and I leave it to you to decide for yourself: if Almighty God gives a man a cowardly pair of legs, how can he help their running away with him?"

*　*　*

He felt that wanton execution of deserting soldiers was not only improper but also damaging to the nation:

"When neither incompetency, nor intentional wrong, nor real injury to the service is imputed—in such cases it is both cruel and impolitic, to crush the man and make him and his friends permanent enemies to the administration, if not to the government itself."

✿ ✿ ✿

A one-legged soldier on crutches asked for some kind of a job; he had lost his leg in battle. "Let me look at your papers," said Lincoln. The man had none; he supposed his word was good. "What! No papers, no credentials, nothing to show how you lost your leg! How am I to know that you lost it in battle, or did not lose it by a trap after getting into somebody's orchard?" The President had a droll look on his face. The workingman turned soldier earnestly muttered excuses. Lincoln saw that this man was no regular place-seeker. Most of them came with papers too elaborately prepared. The chances were entirely in favor of any one-legged man having lost his leg in battle. "Well, it is dangerous for an army man to be wandering around without papers to show where he belongs and what he is, but I will see what can be done." Then he wrote a card for the man to take to a quartermaster who would attend to his case.

✿ ✿ ✿

Lincoln was driven to the camp of the 69th New York (Irish), who had fought with impetuous valor and whose Colonel Michael Corcoran was taken prisoner in the thick of the fighting. "Mr. Lincoln made the same feeling address," wrote Sherman, "with more personal allusions, because of their special gallantry in the battle under Corcoran." Here Lincoln again made his offer to hear willingly the grievance of any man. An officer stepped forward who had that morning tried to quit the service and leave camp, with Sherman growling that he would shoot him like a dog. He said: "Mr. President, I have a cause of grievance. This morning I went to speak to Colonel Sherman, and he threatened to shoot me." Lincoln queried, "Threatened to shoot you?" "Yes, sir, he threatened to shoot me."

Lincoln looked at the officer, looked at Sherman, and then, stooping toward the officer as if to give a confidential message, and speaking in a stage whisper that could be heard for yards around, "Well, if I were you, and he threatened to shoot, I would not trust him, for I believe he would do it." The officer turned and vanished.

✿   ✿   ✿

December 26, 1839:

"A witty Irish soldier, who was always boasting of his bravery when no danger was near, but who invariably retreated without orders at the first charge of an engagement, being asked by his Captain why he did so, replied: 'Captain, I have as brave a heart as Julius Caesar ever had; but somehow or other, whenever danger approaches, my cowardly legs will run away with it.'"

✿   ✿   ✿

One Billy Patterson, Mississippi River pilot who was smart at running past Confederate batteries, asked for the captaincy of an old river boat sheeted with iron and mounted with two antiquated guns. A pompous examination committee questioned him about English history and Oliver Cromwell, and Billy Patterson snorted, "I don't know and don't care a damn who he was; I ain't hunting his job." The committee chairman wrote across the application "Not recommended—ignorant and insolent."

Friends took up his case and Lincoln wrote on the back of his application: "This seems to have become a sort of triangular contest between Charles Stuart, Oliver Cromwell and Billy Patterson. It is generally believed hereabouts that Charles and Oliver are dead. If the committee upon investigations finds this to be the fact, give the appointment to Billy Patterson."

STORYTELLING

"I remember a good story when I hear it, but I never invented anything original. I am only a retail dealer."

❖ ❖ ❖

A lady once questioned Lincoln in regard to some of the witticisms attributed to him, mentioning a few of the stock stories. He laughed, and said, "The papers make me smarter than I am. I have said none of these things with one exception. I did say, when I had the small pox, 'Now let the office-seekers come, for at last I have something I can give all of them.'"

❖ ❖ ❖

An Illinois cavalry colonel, John F. Farnsworth, quoted Lincoln on his story-telling:

"Some of the stories are not as nice as they might be, but I tell you the truth when I say that a funny story, if it has the element of genuine wit, has the same effect on me that I suppose a good square drink of whiskey has on an old toper; it puts new life into me. The fact is I have always believed that a good laugh was good for both the mental and the physical digestion."

❖ ❖ ❖

Lincoln often told a story he heard from Alexander Stephens when they were in Congress. It had to do with an undersized lawyer in an acrimonious stump debate with the massive Robert Toombs. Toombs called out, "Why, I could button your ears back and swallow you whole." The little fellow retorted, "And if you did, you would have more brains in your stomach than you ever had in your head."

❖ ❖ ❖

145

"They say I tell a great many stories. I reckon I do; but I have learned from long experience that *plain* people, take them as they run, are more easily influenced through the medium of a broad and humorous illustration than in any other way."

SWEARING

An ambulance took Lincoln, Brooks and some army men for an eight-mile ride out to a corps review. Six mules pulled the coach over a rough road that jolted the passengers. The driver let fly a volley of oaths. Lincoln leaned forward and asked, "Excuse me, my friend, are you an Episcopalian?"

The driver looks around, surprised. "No, Mr. President. I am a Methodist."

"Well, I thought you must be an Episcopalian, because you swear just like Governor Seward, who is a church warden."

✧   ✧   ✧

One of Lincoln's favorite stories:

"It seems there was a colonel who when raising his regiment in Missouri proposed to his men that he should do all the swearing for the regiment. They assented; and for months no instance was known of a violation of the promise. The colonel had a teamster named John Todd, who, as roads were not always the best, had some difficulty in commanding his temper and tongue. John happened to be driving a mule team through a series of mudholes a little worse than usual, when he burst forth into a volley of profanity.

"The colonel took notice of the offense and brought John to account. 'John,' said he, 'didn't you promise to let me do all the swearing for the regiment?' 'Yes, I did, Colonel,' he replied, 'but the fact was the swearing had to be done then or not at all, and you weren't there to do it.'"

TEMPERANCE

Lincoln was asked if he were a temperance man. He replied:

"I am not a temperance man, but I am temperate to this extent: I don't drink."

❖ ❖ ❖

A committee of temperance advocates urged their cause: "The reason we did not win was because our army drank so much whiskey as to bring the curse of the Lord upon them." Lincoln replied it was "rather unfair on the part of the curse, as the other side drank more and worse whiskey than ours did."

❖ ❖ ❖

"Whether or not the world would be vastly benefited by a total and final banishment from it of all intoxicating drinks seems to me not now an open question. Three-fourths of mankind confess the affirmative with their tongues, and, I believe, all the rest acknowledge it in their hearts . . . When there shall be neither a slave nor a drunkard on earth—how proud the title of that land which may truly claim to be the birthplace and the cradle of those revolutions that shall have ended in that victory. How nobly distinguished that people who shall have planted and nurtured to maturity both the political and moral freedom of their species."

❖ ❖ ❖

Lincoln and Tad rode on a white river steamer down the Potomac. Grant, with Colonel Horace Porter and others, went to see Lincoln in the after cabin. Grant said, "I hope you are very well, Mr. President."

"Yes, I am in very good health, but I don't feel very comfortable after my trip last night on the bay. It was rough, and I was considerably shaken up. My stomach has not yet entirely recovered from the effects."

A wiseacre interposed: "Try a glass of champagne, Mr. President. That is always a certain cure for seasickness."

Lincoln eyed him a moment. "No, my friend. I have seen too many fellows seasick ashore from drinking that very stuff."

THE UNION

On the Nebraska Act:

"But Nebraska is urged as a great Union-saving measure. Well, I too go for saving the Union. Much as I hate slavery, I would consent to the extension of it rather than see the Union dissolved, just as I would consent to any *great* evil, to avoid a *greater* one."

"Let us re-adopt the Declaration of Independence, and, with it, the practices and policy which harmonize with it. Let North and South—let all Americans—let all lovers of liberty everywhere—join in the great and good work. If we do this, we shall not only have saved the Union, but we shall have so saved it as to make and to keep it forever worthy of the saving. We shall have so saved it that the succeeding millions of free happy people, the world over, shall rise up and call us blessed to the latest generations."

(1854)

❈ ❈ ❈

On the balcony of Bates House in the chill of a February twilight Lincoln looked out on 20,000 people and told them their reception was certainly no compliment to him personally, but only to him "as a mere instrument, an accidental instrument" of a great cause. Not until he got to Washington would he attempt a lengthy speech. Now he ventured:

"I will only say that to the salvation of the Union there needs but one single thing—the hearts of a people like yours. When the people rise in mass in behalf of the Union and the liberties of this country, truly may it be said, 'The gates of hell cannot prevail against them.' In all trying positions in which I shall be placed, and doubtless I shall be placed in many such, my reliance will be upon you and the people of the United States; and I wish you to remember, now and forever, that it is your business, and not mine; that if the Union of these States and the liberties of this people shall be lost, it is but little to any one man of fifty-two years of age, but a great deal to the thirty millions of people who inhabit these United States, and to their posterity in all coming time. It is your business to rise up and preserve the Union and liberty for yourselves, and not for me. I appeal to you again to constantly bear in mind that not with politicians, not with Presidents, not with office-seekers, but with you, is the question: Shall the Union and shall the liberties of this country be preserved to the latest generations?"

✿ ✿ ✿

Secretary Chase made a long and elaborate constitutional argument against a proposed greenback issue. "Chase," said Lincoln, "down in Illinois I was held to be a pretty good lawyer, and I believe I could answer every point you have made, but I don't feel called upon to do it. This thing reminds me of a story I read in a newspaper the other day. It was of an Italian captain, who ran his vessel on a rock and knocked a hole in her bottom. He set his men to pumping and he went to pray before a figure of the Virgin in the bow of the ship. The leak gained on them. It looked at last as if the vessel would go down with all on board. The captain, at length, in a fit of rage at not having his prayers answered, seized the figure of the Virgin and threw it overboard. Suddenly the leak stopped, the water was pumped out, and the vessel got safely into port. When docked for repairs, the statue of the Virgin Mary was found stuck head-foremost in the hole."

"I don't see, Mr. President, the precise application of your story," said Mr. Chase.

"Why, Chase, I don't intend precisely to throw the Virgin Mary overboard, and by that I mean the Constitution, but I will stick it in the hole if I can. These rebels are violating the Constitution to destroy the Union. I will violate the Constitution, if necessary, to save the Union, and I suspect, Chase, that our Constitution is going to have a rough time of it before we get done with this row."

THE WAR

Speaking to a Quaker woman:

"If I had had my way, this war would never have been commenced."

＊　＊　＊

Between inauguration and the firing on Fort Sumter, he said of the trials of that time: "They were so great that could I have anticipated them I could not believe it possible to survive them."

＊　＊　＊

He did not enter the war with an idea of freeing the slaves:

"My paramount object in this struggle is to save the Union and is not either to save or destroy slavery.

＊　＊　＊

"The fiery trial through which we pass will light us down (in honor or dishonor) to the latest generation."

＊　＊　＊

"Yet, if God wills that it continue until all the wealth piled by the bond-man's two hundred and fifty years of unrequited toil shall be sunk, and until every drop of blood drawn with the lash shall be paid by another drawn with the sword, as it was said three thousand years ago, so still it must be said, 'the judgments of the Lord, are true and righteous altogether.' "

＊　＊　＊

As a metaphor for the hour, Lincoln remarked:

"We are like whalers who have been on a long chase. We have at last got the harpoon into the monster, but we must now